# yooper poetry

# yooper poetry

*On Experiencing Michigan's Upper Peninsula*

Edited by
**Raymond Luczak**

Modern History Press
Ann Arbor, MI

**Reprints**

Raymond Luczak's "Chipmunk" appeared in *Laurel Review* (Issue 55.1, 2022).
Gala Malherbe's "I Look for You" appeared in her chapbook *No One Told Me* (2019).
Beverly Matherne's "The Vision of Eziel" appeared in *Here: Women Writing on Michigan's Upper Peninsula* (Michigan State University, 2015).
R. H. Miller's "Economy" appeared in *A Long Glance* (Finishing Line Press, 2010).
Dana Richter's "Time of the Blackflies" appeared in *The Brockway Lookout* (Vol. 22, No. 2, 2015) and "The Warbling Vireo" appeared in *The Brockway Lookout* (Vol. 27, No. 1, 2020).




Modern History Press
5145 Pontiac Trail
Ann Arbor, MI 48105

Toll-free: 888-761-6268
Fax: 734-663-6861
E-mail: info@modernhistorypress.com

Web: modernhistorypress.com
Distributed by Ingram (USA/CAN/AU)


**Library of Congress Cataloging-in-Publication Data**

Names: Luczak, Raymond, 1965- editor.
Title: Yooper poetry : on experiencing Michigan's Upper Peninsula / edited by Raymond Luczak.
Description: Ann Arbor : Modern History Press, 2024.
Identifiers: LCCN 2024003158 (print) | LCCN 2024003159 (ebook) | ISBN 9781615997930 (paperback) | ISBN 9781615997947 (hardcover) | ISBN 9781615997954 (epub)
Subjects: LCSH: American poetry--Michigan. | Upper Peninsula (Mich.)--Poetry. | American poetry--21st century. | LCGFT: Poetry.
Classification: LCC PS571.M5 Y66 2024 (print) | LCC PS571.M5 (ebook) | DDC 811.540809774--dc23/eng/20240315
LC record available at https://lccn.loc.gov/2024003158
LC ebook record available at https://lccn.loc.gov/2024003159

**Yooping It Up: A Quick Foreword ... i**

***

**Kathleen M. Heideman ... 1**

Now Playing | Miss Iron Range Sings Reba | Father Vaaramäki's Homily |
Poor Rusty, He Was Always Somebody's Weary Young Husband Broken, Dying Early |
Olson Bros. Waste Management | An Educational Program Concerning Mining

**R. H. Miller ... 9**

The Drowned Boy | Columbines | Casino at Watersmeet | Night Fishing for Trout |
Cooks Run, Michigan | Economy | The Wreck | One Vision

**Gala Malherbe ... 17**

The Storm | Our Lake | I Look for You |
A Perfect Place to Find Cranberries | Spring in March | What the Doctor Did Not Know

**Suzanne Sunshower ... 25**

60th Birthday Song | Putting the UP in North | Tonight | Snowy Day with Wind |
Brother / Sister | April Ice Storm | Invasion of Bear Shack | In Respect for Spirit Mound

**John Hilden ... 33**

Bad Blood | A Lover of Pageantry | Portent | The Day Comes |
Messiah Complex | Towpath | Stasis | Essence of Hope

**Kathleen Carlton Johnson ... 41**

Hunting Season | Mistress of Information | Two Stones | The River |
Letter to Father, at Sea | Evening in Late Summer

**Russell Thorburn ... 49**

The Bus Driver's Singing "Real Cool Time," an Iggy Pop Song to Keep Himself Awake |
The Fox | A Union Soldier Drifts in His Canoe Toward the Lake Superior Shore |
Beside the Breakwall Near Five-Foot Splashing Waves | At the University Library in Marquette

**Jane Piirto ... 57**

Meteor Showers | Ketchimaki's Farm | Pinecone | Spectre on the Seney Stretch | Iron Man

**B. Harlan Deemer ... 65**

names | half moon at twenty to noon | a sleek, white winter sentence |
ahead of wishful thinking | stomach | slowly rising temperatures | nest

# contents


## Chad Faries ... 73

Teach: Field Trip | Empire | Iron Family Vignettes | 9th Avenue Song and Run

## Ellen Lord ... 81

Unscheduled Guest | North Country Haiku | Ontonagon at Da Noonlight |
A Rain Poem | Lake Effect Sky | A Snow Day (Again) | Hometown | Porcupine Mountain High

## Jonathan Johnson ... 89

Emily the Dōan's Text | Marquette Update | Twenty-Five Miles from Milk |
Two Daughters | Process | Samu as Cutting Wood a Winter Ahead

## Raymond Luczak ... 97

John A. "Curley" Krainak | That One Time I Fell Asleep in the Garden Behind
the Three-Stall Garage | Chipmunk | Here Lies the Body of a Deaf Boy |
Segueing | News Record Printing and Supply | My First History Teacher

## Dana Richter ... 105

Time of the Black Flies | A Mushroom Is a Microscopic Kind of Thing | Rutabaga! |
Mushrooms in the Huron Mountains | The Warbling Vireo | Any Wayside Place

## Jennifer Elen Bríd ... 113

Sorcery | Reverie | Passion | The North Shore | Sweetness, Shared | Sap Season

## Beverly Matherne ... 121

Come Like a Thief | First Snow at Sunrise | The Vision of Eziel | Resurrection

## Martin Achatz ... 129

Bigfoot and Jim Harrison Skinny Dip in Morgan Pond on Father's Day |
Bigfoot's New Year's Resolutions | Bigfoot Meets a Homeless Man on Presque Isle |
Crossing the Straits | Moose | Portrait of the Virgin Mary as Skunk | Doe After a Blizzard

## T. Kilgore Splake ... 137

untitled | god's country | memories | yooper obituary |
keweenaw reflections | of water | yooper samizdat

## Deborah K. Frontiera ... 145

In Search of the Giant Killer | Night Sky | Sounds While Sitting in Silence |
The Crocus Race | Leaving Home


***


## Contributors ... 152

for
Steven Schuster

## Yooping It Up: A Quick Foreword
by Raymond Luczak

Up north, nobody cares for rambling speeches, so I'm not going to pad this one with scholarly distractions and squint-causing footnotes about how poetry can be some sort of a salve against the onslaught of seasons, particularly when it comes to the relentless grip of winter. However I must run the risk of offending those trolls still living under the Mackinac Bridge by explaining what the term "Yooper" means. The acronym for Michigan's Upper Peninsula is "U.P.," and "Yooper" is derived from saying the blended word "U.P.-er" unlike the word "upper." Got that? Awesome!

So let's yoop it up, shall we?

Now, if you're new to the U.P. experience, you must understand that Yoopers, especially those who live there year-round, are *tough*. Those long winters can feel more interminable especially when the first snow arrives with joy in October and lingers like a cold that just won't go away until April. You can bitch and moan all you want, but last night's snowdump of two feet—surprise!—is not going to shovel itself out of the driveway. You just have to don your longjohns (or longjanes), plop your feet into your snowmobile boots, zip up your parka, get your butt out there, and push the big-assed scooper, stockpiling that snowbank which never seems to stop growing until the last gasps of spring.

The funny thing is, despite the tiny icicles dripping from your nose, you find yourself blissfully alive while sipping that marshmallow-laden mug of hot chocolate and feeling the happy wriggling of your toes inside your thick slippers while you watch a sitcom on TV. Sometimes I swear there's nothing better than feeling that slight snap in the night air while sleeping under a weight of blankets; my body feels wonderfully blessed by the heat that's been trapped. Being a Yooper requires the ability to appreciate such small miracles as they occur. In that sense, living in the U.P. could be considered *almost* a spiritual experience.

Given the rigors of winter, the summers there can be shockingly glorious. The hours of sunlight are blissfully long enough to make us forget the previous winter. The lush green everywhere is occasionally punctuated with the most electrifying thunderstorms that leave behind in the air a startling chill, almost like a glass of icy lemonade on a sweltering afternoon. (Well, sometimes you have to learn to ignore those pesky bugs. No wonder that I love the dusky challenge of tracking those bats who gobble up those annoying mosquitoes left and right in the first leak of night. But I digress.)

Many of the poems chosen for inclusion often end with a hard-earned clarity of recognition; it may not always be as warm as a firepit on a cool August night, but it is emotionally honest. Otherwise, poetry might as well be a futile pursuit.

Oh, no no no. We all deserve better.

Some of the poems here allude to the lingering residual power of the mining industry in the U.P. At one time, the Iron Range (and the Copper Country too) brought forth so much iron and copper ore (and lumber, too!) to the world that entire towns, enriched by immigrants from the Old World bringing along their languages, cultural norms, and recipes (well, the Cornish-inspired pasty which has become *the* U.P. dish), seemed to appear out of nowhere along with the riches for the owners of the mining companies. Then the deposits of such ore did eventually run dry, so the towns shrank accordingly. Thankfully, Mother Nature hasn't left.

While I love nature poetry, I felt that this anthology needed more than that. What about *living* there as a resident? So many of us who've moved away have never forgotten the personal landmarks that loomed large in our formative years. Yes, there is indeed more to life in the U.P. than the powerful rhythm of its seasons. All the poets in this collection have been given approximately eight pages each. This enables us to savor their work more intimately as one might with making a new friend.

Well, that's all I've needed to say, folks. Welcome to da U.P. and enjoy!

**Now Playing**

Down at the Delft Theater we're all watching that silent film, *Taming the Michigan Wilderness*, for the umpteenth time. When it's done, the projectionist plays it backwards, to rewind, & everyone stays to watch that too, even better, like it was a vaudeville Magician's act—O how astonishing!—to see our black trains running backwards uphill from the oredocks, engines swallowing smoke, broken ore pouring out from trams, back down shaft-holes where it came from, our grandfathers unbent & growing younger, smiling now, the roads un-ribboning, replaced by ferns & upholstered slopes of pin-cushion moss, the Miner's Bank & Trust building dissembled, dragged stone by stone back to the quarry & best of all, great logs rolling uphill from the riverbanks, bouncing a few times like boys on a diving board, and bounding upright: White Pines! White Pines! Wild-haired virgins! Pine trees, ancient trees, far as the eye can see!

kathleen m. heideman

## Miss Iron Range Sings Reba

*How you done me wrong,*
*Baby crank it up!*
*Until you blow the speakers out your Chevy truck.*
                    —Reba McEntire, "Turn on the Radio"


Come Sunday, Rusty, we'll stroll
along the Caving Grounds fenceline
down to Rautamäki Senior Center,
grab ourselves empty folding chairs
—saving this for anybody? No?
It's a creaky end to wondering at last
who'll win the local talent contest,
who'll be named *least likely to escape*
*a collapsing town's gravitational field,*
who'll be crowned *Miss Iron Range*:
most likely not your favorite niece
the one with straight As, braced teeth
and a job at the library, more likely
the neighbor's feral grandchild,
a blonde girl rough as beachgrass
wasting her summer swatting fish-flies,
oiling herself on lakeshore sand
in earshot of the ore dock's rumbling
freighters and the sooty coal yard,
a pre-melanoma case whose special talent
is brazen flirting, opening zippers with her lips
and lip-syncing along to the radio—
she sings Reba, singing loud, singing flat,
and when she blows the words she just laughs
like she's not on stage, like she's flying
down the road with her hair out the window
spit-polishing dust from her tin tiara,
flip-flops propped on a new boy's pickup
dash, her toenails painted black.


                    

## Father Vaaramäki's Homily

Poor Negaunee, so pure with snow, freshly white-washed, so studded with taverns and steeples and shaft heads, iron-stained as any butcher shop, and Father Vaaramäki*, who meant to say "sacrament" tonight and stood there blank-tongued in the middle of the mass, dumbstruck, moonlight leaking from every hole in his head. Silent minutes passed; we worried he was having a stroke—then he opened his mouth and homily poured out: O how the iron range glows and shimmers in Thy falling snow, luminous with well-scrubbed faithful, the white-sugared optimism of mine workings, ore dusted with snow! Must I mention failure or fracture here, this blessed night? I say no! No. For even X waits to deliver bad news, even catastrophe demurs, hangs back like a wolf at the edge of a clearing until Thy deer have ponded like Job floundering in deep snow. Progress! Optimism! Open the ledgers of Industry! Boughs greening our mantles while outside, the spruce grouse thrums and chews her meager needles! Bring out sour black bread and break it, share Thy bounty, Thy juustua and blood-sausages and pickled pig's feet! Thy wine is sweet, Thy wind is bitter. Let bacon-drippings be spread on sacramental wafers for every poor man tonight, and poor babes too, for it is Christmas Eve, a rare full moon swoops low to smile upon our town—grant now our dumb beasts the gift of speech, let the cow and kitten deliver prophecies, let the rooster forecast profits in the coming year, X-many million tons of ore shipped, X-many stopes emptied, X-many cracked streets. Now let us raise our voice in prayer, let us crank the Victrola and sing, for when we sing we are not poor, we are not hollowed, we are holy! And if we cannot be holy, let us cross ourselves and be certain—in X's name we tremble, in X's name make amends.

---

* Finnish words—*vaara* means "danger" and *mäki* means "hill" translated by Teppo Pihlajamäki

k a t h l e e n   m .   h e i d e m a n

## Poor Rusty, He Was Always Somebody's Weary Young Husband Broken, Dying Early

You can't avoid him. Orangey-soda-bright-acid-pyritic
he puddles at your feet, omnipotent; Rusty's face on your beater pickup's
fender oxidizing into brittle lace, he was here from the start,
brittle photos of Rusty double-jacking in Jackson pit, 1856,
prying rock-pages open with his pick, holding drill or shovel,
carbide lamp, his black pupils swelling to fill the whole of his eyes,
O they swore *he could see in the dark, that fellow!*
                              He's there, dumping cantilevered
ore-carts down in the Negaunee, compressed air in Blueberry,
electrified mucker in the Mather B, running the sump engine,
shouldering a widow-maker, and when the final shift
resurfaced, Rusty rode away atop the last orecar
sent downhill to waiting freighters; he swallowed darkness
in every drift he worked, unquenchable thirst that boy, he stood
your grandfather whiskey for whiskey in the Crow Bar
then steered the old man home, he's always been our dearest hope,
our North Star, sacrificial lamb, cherubic choirboy scrubbed for Mass
despite his fading black eye—& inside his work glove
a finger rock-shattered and bloody
                              O he kept going, poor Rusty,
he was always somebody's weary young husband
broken, dying early, dismissed heart-attack, trussed double-hernia
whistling cheery as the men descended single-file in Maas Mine,
into Athens Mine's dark maw, he was our virgin gulleted whole,
boy given night after night to Vulcan Mine, plaything for the town bully,
scapegoat, hero, Miner of the Year—
                              undaunted, tireless,
with a lift of his chin he'd nod to old blind Tiresias, the mine's night watchman
who nightly dug a ruddy trench in shattered hematite to pour the blood libation
fresh from Salo's Meats, raw aperitif to appease the ghosts
who made those wild ore-howls all the miners heard below,
rock-popping-tap-tapping-gnawing noises,
the secret shivering certainty of something deeper
than the lowest level, O, that was Rusty for you, whistling

                         —O he shrugged it off,
never wept, or wept openly, or maybe it was Rusty from the start,
Rusty who made such unearthly sounds, him in the sobbing seams of our heart.

kathleen m. heideman

## Olson Bros. Waste Management

Joke was they managed the waste by merely sorting
junk by type: fridge-stoves this pile, sofa-chairs that,

glass-cans-window-barrels, a billion parts nobody'd take for scrap,
—o, but their genius was in knowing this land like the back

of their hand, unmarked shafts the hidden piggybanks where anything
they dropped stayed down, *abracadabra.* Ka-ching! You'd do the same—

myriad Empire boys sent away for magic coins, rings, brochures,
kits that promised to impart the Art of Making Stuff Disappear!

You'd start small at first, sure: a few bright coins behind your ear,
silk scarves, cards, bags of wormy crab-apples, hardened house paint,

working your way up to shingles, beds, tarp-shrouded loads,
hell, some old widower nobody'd miss, *there's bottomless holes*

Paavo swore, drinking brandy, *if you just know where to look*
and his brother kicked him hard under the bar. *We're Waste Professionals,*

said Ole, his soft hands folded smoothly as a funeral director's,
perfect nails. *It's magic, boys. We wave our wands, make shit go Poof.*

**kathleen m. heideman**

## An Educational Program Concerning Mining

*Here's how it works*, our leader says, picks people from the audience at the Iron Mining History Museum, sorts us by height, makes everybody lift their arms straight out in the air. Our aligned row of necks and our upright spines he calls the *Mine Shaft*. Our parallel lifted arms he calls *Drifts on Consecutively Deeper Levels*. Some mines, he tells us, went down a hundred levels, several thousand feet or more. The tallest fellow's head is the shaft house, his ears are *iron wheels* grooved for hoisting cables. He is ordered to *whistle & squeal & screech*. Fathers are chosen to use their bare hands as *shovels & picks*. The rest of us wait with arms upraised, standing there like we're surrendering. Our leader tells us to send up iron, we must use our hearts, arteries, biceps, stoop and lift, shovel and fill, hammer and blast. *Are you feeling it? It's a hard work, it's a messy business, ore!* A few of our fathers are told to lay down on the floor now, *injured or killed, crushed*, and our leader runs through tossing something between our feet, toy mice made from scraps of rabbit fur. *Rats, everywhere you looked there were rats!* he yells. He's excited now, blowing red dust over us, powdered blood meal. We inhale it and cough. We're sweating now, shouting and squealing and blasting and shoveling and hoisting, waving arms and stooping, red dust caking on wet skin. The audience looks uneasy. *You're the Location, the neighborhood around the mine*, he tells them. He throws red dust on them. *See, red was orebody, red was labor*. He says men died *wheezing, red lung*, he says *Millions of Tons. Billions! Fame & fortune! Are you listening? Are you getting this? Laundry drying on the line turned pink, we took our rock and turned it into Money!* A girl in the audience is weeping, a woman objects, but too late. *Proud history*, says our leader. He gives our fathers scrip, takes it back again. He sells them candles and blasting caps. He plants our mothers here and there, he calls them *virgin pines*, makes them chant *Pines hold up the Mines!*—limbs jutting, limbs akimbo, tossing wild hair, snapping under pressure. The leader says we must cut down our mothers to make more mining timbers. *I didn't ask for this*, whimpers a boy covered with dust; him and his grandmother coughing, rubbing eyes. *We must think about what Industry needs*. The leader tells the children to join hands now, teaches them to sing, *There's a Treasure in the Ground, Dig it Out, Dig it Out! There's a Treasure in the Ground—Dig it Out!* They repeat it jumping up and down in their seats, coughing and stomping their feet while we, a mining machine made of fathers and mothers and children—*Dig it Out, Dig it Out*—go on shoveling and grinding and sweating, shuddering and blasting and suffering. *Dig it Out!*—not sure how we got into this or how we make it stop.

## The Drowned Boy
*In memory of Stephen Machwart**

"So absolute the Deep." —Michael Drayton


Below me, staring up,
in tangled seaweed I find you,
drowned boy, with your undulating golden hair,
like Lycidas, lying in cold splendor
asleep among a million stones
that sparkle in this autumn sun.

My search is ended.  Brother, I come
to touch with living fire
the intertwining helix, and conjure you
to rise through the green wreaths that cover you,
clasp my hands and walk with me.

Within those eyes that draw me down
to the blue water I see myself,
flapping my arms like some helpless drunk.
The drowned boy rocks stiffly side to side.
He lifts his bloated arms to embrace me
and floats slowly up,
beckoning.

_______________

* Stephen was the son of a neighbor in Houghton; in June 1961, he drowned in a sailing accident
in Lake Superior.

## Columbines

*Forest Hill Cemetery, Houghton, Michigan*

Washed out pale after years of blooming
the columbines now fragile grip
the earth with a pioneer's strength
for they know what it is to suffer
as she did through her firstborn's death
a baby lovely as a columbine's soft creamy blossom
tinged with violet nestled in fringed green.
Too soon blown too soon faded precious child.
Lovely yet she not so strong not so rooted
in the earth so fixed in life.
The child is gone but the delicate blossoms
abide whispering in the wind we are here
you live in us forever.

**Casino at Watersmeet**

A cold wind sweeps the parking lot.
The metallic sky tells me
there's a storm coming.
Cars gleam shiny and new
but show pits of rust where
Michigan's winter has corroded
the brittleness of their psychedelic coats.
Inside the casino rockabilly blares
and cigarette smoke and the reek
of stale beer and burgers pollute
the aisles like a sulfurous fog.
Poker machines flash like
sequined whores hustling.
Invalids in wheelchairs
others with their walkers
at the ready stare at
the tempting screens.
Outside the wind blows over
trees where dead stalks
of ironweed rattle a voodoo cadence.
From deep in the woods
a lone partridge beats
a tattoo on a hollow log
Thump-thump thump-thump-thump.

r. h. miller

## Night Fishing for Trout
*Somewhere on the Otter River*

Sweat trickles into my eyes.
Damp shirt clings to my skin.
Leaves rustle in my ear their
jagged edges scratch my face.
One foot in front of another
I probe the bottom for purchase
among hidden rocks like
bowling balls sudden drop-offs
treacherous brush falls.
A bat snares my fly on
the back cast.  Trembling
shrieking it comes loose
and flutters off black into black.
Between overhanging tag alders
arching from each bank I cast
my fluttering hex fly
bone white into a pool of ink.
On the long blind float
back toward me about six feet
out a startling KERSHLUNK!
I yell out Holy Shit!
The line twangs like a banjo string.
My rod arcs near breaking
and then the line goes slack.
I quake like a boy at First Confession
gather my wits and line
and say to anyone listening
Thank God.

**Cooks Run, Michigan**

Tucked away between tag alders
rippling over cobblestones
and pebbles colored like
a crazy quilt it is home
to brook trout and browns
dotted in blues and reds
darting through glassy pools
and to silk-wing mayflies
that on warm summer evenings
ascend in clouds skyward
from glittering surfaces
and also home to fly fishers
who find in its healing waters
what they are looking for
and lose what in life they wish
they had not found.

**Economy**

My grandfather was buried without pants.
My grandmother told me what was the point
if he was on view only from the waist up.
So he lay looking quite dignified
but to me slightly absurd if you can
imagine what it is like to go
to your Eternal Rest having forgotten
to put on your pants.
That was only one of his economies.
It was our habit when the butchering
was done to call on Stormy Brinkman
our neighbor down the road
to kill the hogs in return for which
he got a panful of fresh pork liver.
An economy but not really since it was
a delicacy that only few people today
can appreciate.  It was so fresh it
rivaled the tastiest calves liver
poached in clarified butter and sherry
and served on toast points.
But then I discovered it was not economy
after all that brought our neighbor
to the killing field but a cry deep
from the heart for Grandpa standing
at the sty with tears in his eyes
so loved his beasts he could not bear
to commit the murderous deed.
Some things we do to save a dollar
some things we do because it is
in us and rises from the soul
and saves without end.

**The Wreck**

I went to see a man about a dog.
He lived like a tornado survivor
in a dilapidated mobile home
but the tornado was of his own making.
He had a yard full of junk
and a black Chevy that sat
on a rusted chassis like
a huge desiccated beetle
on a rotting board.
In and out a passenger window
flew a flock of white-crowned sparrows
in their crisp white-and-black caps
chirping to the brightening day
like a choir of nuns at matins.
A professor of mine once said
that art ought to improve
on nature but there
on that slovenly acre
it was a comfort to know
that nature in its smallest gesture
can redeem the world we have made.

**One Vision**

On a gloomy morning
two sojourners in a boat
floating down a murky river
mythic spooky wait
for something to appear
out of the thickening mist.
The old man sits astern looks ahead
while the boy sits amidships
handles the rowing
looks beyond the old man to see
if anything is following them.
The old man sees ahead to perils
yet to come calls out
cues to guide the boat
through submerged rocks trees
while the boy scans
dangers they have avoided.
Deep deep in the miasma
the boy sees the old man sees
the boy.  In each other they see
both past and future
swirl into one vision
of what is to come
of what has been.

**The Storm**

I was probably doing somersaults underwater
or swimming out past the drop-off with sisters and cousins
when those ominous clouds moved in from the north,
high and layered, traced in charcoal.
We watched them swallow the sun,
felt the chill of low winds crossing water
as mother summoned us with open beach towels,
wrapped our goose pimpled, sun-brown bodies in terry cloth.
By the time I reached our camper,
my bare feet were slippered in mud.
The sky flickered yellow. Leaves blew upside down.
Dad secured the boat, covered the wood pile,
rolled up the windows on the truck
as the first heavy drops pelted the tin roof.
We huddled together on cushioned bench seats, hair still dripping,
watched the lake fill with circles, saw the dry earth leap,
listened as the rumble moved closer,
imagined God and his angels bowling in the folds of that dark sky,
heard that shiny marbled ball heavy on the alley,
the crash of giant pins, each time a little closer to the flicker,
a little closer to our campsite, a little closer
to our wide eyes, to our small pounding hearts.
Each time the sky split open with light, we waited, fists clenched,
*One thousand one, one thousand two …*
until there was no time between the flash and the noise.
That final crack felt like an emergency or an accident,
sounded like a universe ending or beginning,
or maybe trees exploding.
After the storm, we found the human size splinters
jabbed in the ground like darts, smelled the burnt marrow of maple.
But that hemlock on the hill did not explode
when lightning licked its highest boughs.
It channeled that strike from top to bottom
as electricity sliced through bark and cambium like a skill saw.
We can still slide our fingers through that groove.

**Our Lake**

I can still hear the wail of loons in the calm air of early morning,
feel the heat of late July after dinner, sun beating on our eastern shore,
staining our faces golden. I see the dome of endless stars above us,
the bats swooping, flashlights at the command of small hands
scanning the shallows for crayfish, as we huddle around the last embers
of a fire no one wants to leave.


I can still see Uncle Rick bounding out fully clothed, diving into the lake
just to make us laugh. I feel my grandmother's hands and comb on my scalp,
dividing and weaving my lake-damp hair into braids. I smell our pine bough
    forts,
feel the sting of cuts on my palms from picking the bracken fern.
I see my father's silhouette in his boat, his hand on the motor at sunset
as he heads out, leaves a trail of silver-rose ripples in his wake.

**I Look for You**

I look for you in the waves

that swell and crest like your laughter,
like your laughter as you watched our cat dart,
arch-backed in his kitten gallop to climb the couch and walls,
to pounce at your feet in a frenzy,
like your laughter as you pointed at our dog nuzzling for frogs,
nose buried in tall grasses, ears perked up curious,
as he pawed the shallows where they escaped him
all afternoon in long leg streaks of green,
their bubble eyes blinking, their throats full of air,
like your laughter that mixed with the wind and the water
the day you stood barefoot in the sand,
holding hands with your sister, pant legs rolled to knees,
the two of you watching for whitecaps, squealing
as you crouched, leapt in unison,
landed in the pulling retreat of swirling surf,
breathless, and waited for the next.

I look for you in the trees

as they stand blushing, spill tamarack tears
in a halo of gold on grass still green.
I follow the pure line of the birch,
follow that painted fork like a map, hope it will lead me
to your unflinching brown eyes, your round freckled nose,
to the soft baby hairs that swirl blond on the back of your neck.
I hope it will lead me to your mittened hand on a Friday morning,
holding tightly to my own as we walk the 8 blocks to school,
as we count cats in windows and on porches,
as we recite spelling words, and follow the cardinal's shrill yodel,
find that bright beating heart in the branches.

I look for you in this field

where I stand unprotected from November's coming,
remember the flock of snow buntings that surprised us,
how they rose up like a breath of fog, white and glinting,
how you told me they looked like fish,
the silver ones that swim together in a bunch,
how on that day we stood frozen, heads tipped skyward,
flew with that arctic flock until a single bunting broke our trance,
spiraled up alone from the grass,
disappeared into the hands of the tallest oak.
We wondered if they'd find him,
wondered if he'd go searching for his flock.

And now, as I stand here looking for you,

I understand that it was you
in that feather wisp of a being,
hiding in the camouflage of your field,
that you have risen freely,
are perched in the branches of your journey,
and that even as you spread your wings on the wind,
your eyes follow that glittering flock,
that piece of sky held open,
that you see the space between wing beats
and know that it will always belong to you.

**A Perfect Place to Find Cranberries**


We were woozy with delight
that night in the restaurant, after the reading,
crowded around tables. We told stories
the way poets do, listened and swooned
with laughter, paused, hands on hearts,
over the good fortunes and misfortunes of life,
sipping chardonnay and pale ale.

I talked of my foraging, how I waited now
for the cranberries. You talked of your bog,
where you saw the heron, a silver minnow
still fresh in his beak, where through your window
you watched a deer bow down to drink.

Oh, the colors! We celebrated—
the golden glow of tamaracks,
the green-violet pitcher plants, cotton flowers,
whimsical like snow, black mud waiting
to squeeze around rubber boots, swallow
each step into sponge, into sieve.

We made a giddy plan.
We would go to your bog, find cranberries
beneath November gray,
ripe and red after the first frost.
We'd pick until our fingers numbed,
fill our basket with rose firm fruit,
a forage to close the year.

I saw you at the Market in December.
I asked about the cranberries.
You blushed, replied that there weren't any after all,
that you'd only imagined them to be there.
We laughed and understood
that the gift had been in the dreaming,

gala malherbe

but it really had seemed
like a perfect place to find cranberries.

## Spring in March

A finch sits on the shovel handle,
waits for his turn at the thistle-filled socks
that hang and sway with the slight weight
of a dozen hungry birds—
goldfinch, siskins, redpoll.
There's a chickadee at the window feeder.
March is brutal today, full of wind and fury.
Late season snow asks us again for resilience.
Yesterday, robins on the farm fields
found food in patches of sun-thawed earth.
Yesterday our tires and tennis shoes
gripped sidewalks and asphalt
while snow slipped away in small rivers,
followed curbs into gutters, quenched
our spring-thirsty spirits with puddles.

gala malherbe

**What the Doctor Did Not Know**

The doctor that delivered the news
to my father and me that day,
the news about his broken lungs,
did not know that my dad was not done living,
that he would still sing, even if
his voice was weak and hoarse,
play his guitar, even if
his wrists were red and swollen,
that he would sneak outside to hang laundry
when my mom was not at home,
that he would take a chance and remove it all—
oxygen cord, wrist brace, walker,
for one cool, poignant leap in the lake.
The doctor did not know that my dad
would take his oxygen tank
to the blueberry patch, rig it with 25 feet of tubing,
crawl on hands and knees
until his hamstrings ached,
pick four quarts of blueberries in three hours.
The doctor did not know that my dad
was not done living, that he had no pride
in how things looked or seemed,
only a fierce enthusiasm for the gifts of his life.
The doctor did not know that my dad
would choose to become breathless if it meant
saying thank you to the receptionist,
calling her by name, or pausing to shake hands
with the man who said, *Welcome home brother*,
that my dad would still go camping, fishing,
side-by-side riding, and putz in the basement.

## 60th Birthday Song

*(said to friends upon moving to what would become Bear Shack)*

I'll do my sixties my own way,
thank you.
This isn't my first rodeo,
in a forest or anywhere else.

You saw me dancing in the big town
before I tippled on the edge
of a small one. And there was
that hilly Dakota cabin …
as well as mountains, rivers, seas
that I climbed or forded
in between.

You know perfectly well
that I've hopped across many
a creek, stone, and marsh,
to wander woods …

as I continually brought to life
my own imagination.

Now I'm doing it
again.

**s u z a n n e   s u n s h o w e r**

## Putting the UP in North

*(one month into the woods at Bear Shack)*

My mind is an overstuffed appetizer.
I'm new to this.
So much fretting going on ...

Handling the axe safely
and chopping wood—to find
it's rotten. Tending a fire
all night successfully
—but getting no sleep.

Staring at/but avoiding
the chain saw and generator,
because they are above my pay grade
—and luckily, I still don't need them.

So many things on my mind,
to prepare for my first winter here ...
I've been filling up on the small stuff
and missing the meal.

How could I almost not see
how lovely the stars are tonight?
So extraordinarily present in the broad sky
—they are truly no mere snack.

I must put down the mental shrimp fork
that only gathers bits and pieces,
and give my mind a backhand slap.

And remember, too, that I must sometimes
look UP.

**Tonight**
(*four months into the woods at Bear Shack*)


And sometimes it's a lie.
I look up—out here,
but there are no stars.
Only the drip from branches
and a vague mist.
Even the dog seems disappointed,
looking hither and yon,
and then up—as if in last resort,
also wondering: Where
in this wide sky
is our prize tonight?
Resignedly, we trundle back inside
to cuddle up again. At least
we still have ourselves,
and sometimes that's all you get.
Each other.

## Snowy Day with Wind

*(five months into the woods at Bear Shack)*

Winds persist through afternoon.
Snow dust blows from over-powdered trees,
so many small things in a rush at once.
Dog's sugary muzzle tilts up
in usual mask of sincerity.
No match for cuteness, human melts.
No one singing for food now,
both fur and feather hunkered down.
Tree fist-tops shake, more than just a sway.
Human surveys cedar marsh nervously,
notes which trees wobble too much.
A top came down in autumn, over wires—
such danger seems never far.
Before, Michigan's tornado-land mid-section
was scary on its own terms ...
but there's a different take on wind
now, living in a forest.
Majestic beauties, life-givers, warmth
and shelter providers: Trees
are savored best when enjoyed upright,
not so much when crashing down.

## Brother / Sister
*(six months into the woods at Bear Shack)*


*for the Black guy in the parking lot in Sault Ste. Marie*


Oh hey, whoa!
the guy says,
getting out of his car.

I give a Hey back—
and laugh.
We point to each other ...

It's a dual acknowledgment,
from one dark trunk to another
in a sea of birch.

## April Ice Storm

*(six months into the woods at Bear Shack)*

All this shoving
of winter into spring ... trees,
coming and going—glazed masses
break dancing in tune to a roaring sky,
leaves me breathless.
Funny, how much I enjoyed the chilly ride
of winter—who would believe
I don't want Winter to go?
But with this last storm's end
comes Spring—its muddy feet
kicking at my door, uncaring
of my unacceptance, it now demands
I jump on this new ride and take it
wherever it goes.

**Invasion of Bear Shack**
*(ten months into the woods at Bear Shack)*


I still shook, a day later.
Ten months—only thinking of bears,

and battling smaller creatures, but not
having to contend with human approach—

a modern car roared up the dirt path
and parked like it belonged.

I pulled on clothes and hobbled forward,
angry—all friends had been advised

not to surprise me like that. Sudden
company? I just don't live that kind of life.

This ain't no fancy cabin—it's hot or it's cold,
and there's no running water ... at least not inside.

Living with ever-present forest pests,
it's nice to choose my human encounters.

Now there was a couple at my open door ...
the man holding up a tract, telling me about God

not creating evil or wanting me to suffer.
And perhaps to their surprise, I fully agreed.

Then I suddenly began to visibly tremble,
until I finally got them to leave.

If they were so darn holy, why couldn't they tell
how intrusive their presence was to me?

I live alone in the woods, I don't need to be saved.

## In Respect for Spirit Mound
*(twelve months into the woods at Bear Shack)*

What happens here, stays here.
Earthen mound haunted by gnashing teeth
and picked bones lying still—

but never active horror.
Action almost always takes place in the dark
before human and dog reappear.

I stand up tall on Spirit Mound
and look around—honor the energy.
Much death with life happens in these woods.

Today, fresh meaty bones scatter the ground.
Judging by the ribcage size, the grazing skunk
was not the perpetrator this time.

There are no cameras in a forest.
Interlopers cannot know what happens
when an unsuspecting back is turned.

**Bad Blood**

I sense there's a story
that isn't being told
when a friend asks
his dad to slow down
so he can point out
the spot on the road
where the squad car
of an undersheriff
caught fire & burned ...
Either that or the son
has lifted the lid
on a tale not meant
for public consumption
His dad tromps on the gas
knocking us back in our seats

**j o h n   h i l d e n**

**A Lover of Pageantry**

When a prancing horse
emerges from the fog
it seems a lost part
of you has reappeared
You sit like a child
touched in freeze tag
thumb flicking ash
from your cigarette
Asked to mail a letter
when you are five
you drop it between
two porch boards
It was a brass band
that drew you downtown
a pair of skinned knees
that sent you limping home

**Portent**

Homework done, he sits
on the sun porch
peering through binocs
His mother knows
what they say
about apron strings
mollycoddled kids
She rattles pans;
tells him to go outside
It startles her when
he appears at her side
tears welling, telling her
a fledgling has fallen from its nest

**j o h n   h i l d e n**

**The Day Comes**

It happens beneath your notice
The luster of your childhood
has been wearing off
like the nap on the couch
You walk home from school
passing a basketball rim
naked without a net
You feel as overexposed
as the photo taken
by your pixilated aunt:
You stand by the garden gate
picking at a scab on your elbow
It's your final Halloween
You trick or treat in thin disguise:
charcoal mustache, Lone Ranger mask

**Messiah Complex**

When Ronnie walks down
the creek in waders
a stick in each hand
spanking the water
sweeping planted trout
before him like a foe
he thinks he's saving us
from those who come
from other towns
to catch our fish & leave ...
It's the opposite with
the guidance counselor
up at Hilltop High
"There's no money here,"
he says to the sons
& daughters of the town
"Swim downstream
to more prosperous shores."

**Towpath**

A school of minnows turns
as though with one thought
as he stands knee-deep
in water at the beach
As a buckboard speeds us
in an old-time western
its spokes appear to spin
counter-clockwise
He's saving these things
and taking on more
like the kid pictured in
a history textbook
towing a barge on the Erie Canal

**Stasis**

A St. Patty's Day storm
drops two feet of snow
I wake to the news
school's called off
A state of suspension
as I step outside
telephone lines sag
freight of heavy snow
A driver slides down
a steep incline
the car on its nose
leaning against an oak
I try not to disturb
the fragile equilibrium
as like a snowbird I alight
and fly away

john hilden

**Essence of Hope**

I could spend all day thinking
thoughts as black as
those I have peering in
the coal bin attached
to the back of my house ...
I'd rather dwell on the mint
that volunteered after
we tore the coal bin down
its healing scent
as a kid biking down
the alley stopped
and we heard a thump
as an apple fell from the tree
rolling down the slope to my feet

**Hunting Season**

He will appear, after work
going straight to the closet,
pull out a satchel and stuff it,
underwear, socks, pants and shirt.
In a plastic bag, toothbrush, paste and comb.
So focused he cannot speak.

I look as he enters the hall,
the light is dim, but it does not hide,
that distance growing between us.

The walls look geometric
cold in the shadows, his gear waits,
he rummages for his gun downstairs.

What is this that draws him into a wooded place,
to hunt and sleep amongst other males.
The primitive becomes evident.

Our homely exchanges rotate
around groceries, socks, and misplaced hats.
There is only one direction
and that is urgent.
The mandatory kiss
and he never looks back.

I have lost the person I love to a wolf's heart,
but say nothing, as expected of the wife.
For two weeks our lives stop,
sadness and sinking rotate in awkward waves.

When he returns, smelling of woodstove,
bacon grease, and sweat.
When he has showered and melted back into
the family, he will be happy,

kathleen carlton johnson

greeting me as his wife,
and we will continue.

42

**Mistress of Information**

My education
awash in competition
all roads leading to the library,
where Miss T resided with her books,
shelved according to category
rotating magazines to newer versions
processing lists of timely loans.

Her penny loafer/cardigan style
mistaken by other students as plainness
and repetition in manner
was calculated management
teetering between exquisite balance of
citizenship, deportment, and ladylike behavior.
A Caribbean spirit
had defused its natural self
years before in exotic Bermuda
holidays of skilled entertainment.
Long narratives that always contained lost luggage, slender waists
and demure poses from a bar stool.

Ages had passed since Mother had seen to it
that lively memories of island affection were exchanged
for virginal books, all in correct Dewey order.
She was pressed into a private school
teaching Grammar,
the sticky stuff of sentences.

It was my first sway into her realm,
dressed in a blue blazer,
with the imprint of the school's crest
in the same spot where my heartbeat
close to my chest.
Education, I was learning,
was perfect attendance

kathleen carlton johnson

and achievement inscribed
on a bronze auditorium plaque.

**Two Stones**

We have decided to become
two stones, side by side,
cast into the sea,
boiling downward, to the bottom
resting in silty gray.

Will we be satisfied,
drinking in the sea,
the sun somewhere above?

What shall we say,
nestled in each other's arms?
With water so fragile and tender,
can we endure the salt?

**The River**


If it is just about water
I could answer the question.
The floating and rapid
growth of pools after rain
or the mud that blackens the hull
as we pull to the shore.

Rivers, however, are usually
sandy bottomed, silt lined
stone filled with random fish.

It is the stories a river tells
between the banks,
river bends, sand bars,
the occasional sunken log,
boys jumping to swim,
merchandise going to market.

Water crossed by a bridge
must now take sides.

The river becomes political.

**Letter to Father, at Sea**


Are you thinking of your little house
from your bed of waves,  the house,
with cathedral ceiling, a fireplace and a small mowed yard ?
do you recall the picnic
or the summer we visited your sister in Michigan
driving all night in a two-toned station wagon ?
as you lean on the rail, one foot on the second row of chain links,
 the sliding sea beneath your feet.
A drenching wind passes,  you do not smoke,
it is silent  except for  constant pulse of the engines.


I write to tell you, we miss your reliable leadership,
behaving as minors, we could be more involved
but we adjust the drapes so it is private at home.
all  three of your daughters are taught adoration,
the  Magnolia  perfuming through the front picture window,
repairs some of the damage of living in yet, another  place.


Mother has not resisted with arguments,
either social or educational .
home is home and worthy of gratitude.
we are  accessories,  keeping  the nation safe.
loyal to your home comings, every  8 months or so.
when you arrive, when the fleet comes home,
we  polish floors and make immaculate order,
we have grown to love the time we take between ,
blot out the farewells, the iron ramp that holds the dock,
To the ship where you climb and salute,
 asking permission to go aboard,
we are amazed at your crispy military dress,
        like the flag, proud.


We light a candle for your protection and return, Father,
 so you may resume activities
        in the home you have provided.

kathleen carlton johnson

## Evening in Late Summer

It happens in summer sometimes,
stillness where the clouds like bread
for ducks have been thrown
on the sky; perfection suspending
us in the universal pond
where small fish watch
a humid moon, riding in the clouds,
rising in thunderheads to the west.

Trees are breath between bodies
pressing hollow bark,
dark brown and gray as an owl.
We have forgotten, though, winter ice
or prison rains that ruin seed.
We have traveled far to see
and wonder if outrage is still
appropriate for slaughter,
as we click our tongues
at a slit earth, root packed,
headed for darkness.

## The Bus Driver's Singing "Real Cool Time," an Iggy Pop Song to Keep Himself Awake

Who knows when we will stop
and I nudge my girlfriend who's not awake
to tell her about the junkie
in the back row shouting at the deer
standing in the middle of the snowy
road with its deep drifts: one lane
to let us pass into the blizzard.

I should let her sleep eight hours,
but the bus driver hasn't quit singing
ever since we left Escanaba;
he's taken it upon himself to punk
out on "I Wanna Be Your Dog"
by Iggy and The Stooges; his black hands
gripping the steering wheel
as if he was back in Detroit.

After reading under my private light,
not knowing what else to do
and unable to sleep like my girl, I look
down again at the blurry ink
of Rainer Rilke's poem about a panther.
I feel that I have become his restless animal
in my seat, wondering when this time
on the bus will free us from our cage.

The junkie in the back is a boy
with needle marks; we saw him board the bus,
already skating from withdrawal
in Escanaba, at the bowling alley
that was the bus station.

He's agitated now, maybe at another
animal that darts as if it was never there

on the road, or where he's going
below the Bridge will just be more pain
for his addiction: a bad dream
as the snowy miles spin up under the tires
and the taint in his blood runs too thin.

It doesn't help the black bus driver,
burly and grasping the steering wheel,
keeps singing more Stooges: "Real Cool Time."
We miss another animal frozen
in our headlights, and the junkie
with his needle arm roams the aisle,
touching each passenger.

Up from his seat, his Detroit stage,
he pounces upon the boy, and points
to a glimmering scene of road and Lake Michigan
in existential fury during the storm.
He rests his hands on his shoulders,
whispering in that Lou Rawls kind of way,
there's nowhere else to go but outside.

The junkie boy finally sits down,
our next stop the food pantry
in St. Ignace, where we will squeeze in
to wait among light bulbs and canned goods,
coffee for us to drink; watch the dawn
in its imitation of day uncover what
was hidden in the dark.

## The Fox

He read the labels on the soup cans,
and his eyes, dark and hungry, looked
up at the checker girl who stood
in awe of this fox who knew he'd
return to his den in the woods,
where every bent branch or smell
taught him only he was an animal
who foundered sometimes in the wind
and went hungry during the night.
The checker girl showed her age
like a dirty sleeve rubbed over
too much makeup. She tapped
her foot and swung her hips
like some crazy clock chiming midnight.
She walked down the deli aisle
to select lunch, and saw herself
staring back from the hot cases
where the mashed potatoes
lay in their buttery bed.
The fox with his pointed nose,
sniffed the dinner of her legs,
the chicken pot pie crusted
a golden brown like her hair;
her flesh this melting butter.
The fox was an intelligent animal
and his coat was a similar color
to winter berries and sunsets
aflame over Lake Superior beaches.
He followed the checker girl's hands
as she accepted her egg rolls
and pot pie from an emaciated woman
of no age but old. She picked her
steps carefully not to spill her lunch,
well aware of the fox at her heels,
who lifted his royal tail, aroused,

**russell thorburn**


at her bare legs and locked hips
in this escape upstairs he couldn't go;
fearful of the butcher with his Van Dyke
beard and smock that reeked of animals
who once roamed the earth.

## A Union Soldier Drifts in His Canoe Toward the Lake Superior Shore

The waves against his canoe lull him,
his paddle over his knees, as he returns
to that cloudless day when he wore
blue trousers of the north for McClellan.
The old horses who pulled the cannons
into Miller's Field still churning mud
with their hooves. The shouts of the men
charging through the corn, their harvest
in blood staining the ears.

Wifeless at thirty, he bares his busy
head of hair, uncut since Sharpsburg,
his scraggly sideburns built into a beard,
some of it now tinged with hoar frost,
and lays his cap beside his Bible.
Lord, he might say any time,
his paddle lifted like his mind
to the sky, let the sorrow that hollows
my heart go away, but squinting
into the sun, he knows he hasn't heard God.

He watches his oar shining bloody
in the circled haze of a setting sun
that's foundering into foam,
as his canoe bucks under each wave,
and sees his captain topple from his mare,
his saber clutched like a lightning rod
attracting all those musket shots.
He knows his prayer is only whiskey
once drunk in a tin cup at Sharpsburg.

russell thorburn

**Beside the Breakwall Near Five-Foot Splashing Waves**

Sailboats up on blocks like little hotels
propose a place for ghosts who never
left behind their desire to be free of land.
Moored to the parking lot, they tremble
in the eternal snow of the stars,
their masts rattle with claws
that no longer grip metal: the hull
in its visible stillness forever seen now
for those walking by, who compare
these guestless interiors to their own
secret places where they don't want to be seen
as frozen feet filled with a heavy sorrow
of those who have never left their cabins.

**At the University Library in Marquette**

There it is in her hand about
to be checked out of the library
where you felt like you were a ghost walking
uninhabited aisles upstairs with windows
looking out at the university.
The librarian with her bobbed black hair,
her eyes of espresso, checks you out
too it seems, worthy of a backhanded
stamp; and you are thinking of André Breton
who wanders through your blank pages
not necessarily anything about Marquette
or where you must walk with strange words
in their revolution to become somebody else.
Nobody reads books anymore,
and she marvels at your youthful eyes,
as if they belonged to a surreal pattern
of blocks mapped out in a metropolitan city,
like Paris where you encounter a stranger
with his fingers clenching this volume.
But that person is only you in your Sorel boots,
overdressed for literature with your Carhartt
duck jacket for the rainy day—*Nadja,*
with its ostrich black letters stretching their necks
in the shape of the title and the author's name.
You might meet him on the Boulevard Bonne-Nouvelle,
or at six o'clock when the moon has risen
above the Eiffel Tower. He is hurrying
to the conservatoire for Apollinaire's play,
and in the balcony he will be talking to Picasso.
It is Banned Books Week, and you keep
thinking of your own Nadja, her eyelids carved
from the stone of a Sphinx, or some mythological
personality that only wanted to consume you.
Nadja keeps a certain distance between you,
and advances only if she wants you: picture how

the ink stamper hangs over all the other
due dates that linger like love affairs
that ran out of time. You have selected her today
in the library because the game was to find
a book that revealed to you your past.
You saw *Nadja* of the small Evergreen
original edition from Grove Press,
written by that André Breton
of surreal poetry and a free union
with his wife and her hair of burning splinters,
eyelashes rims of a swallow's nest,
upstairs in the library's darkened aisle.

## Meteor Showers

"What, craftsman, are you preparing there?
What, blacksmith, are you making?"
—Runo 49, *The Kalevala*

The sparks from my father's
welding rods threw showers
of sparks onto the concrete floor
of his shop in the back yard.
He had on a welder's hood.
He stopped the weld,
tossed the hood back.
"Don't look
at the white quivering light.
Look aside
or you'll go blind."

He had a side business.
His union job was
in the Brownstone Shops
of CCI—Cleveland Cliffs Iron.
Evenings he wrought iron,
twisting fences, rails, and gates,
designing and forging stainless steel,
sauna stoves and water tanks
for camps and homes.

I have tried to see a
meteor shower in the night sky
but have not.
I have seen the aurora borealis
but the only meteor showers
I have seen were those

---

* All epigraph quotes come from *The Kalevala* (Translator, Francis Peabody Magoun). Harvard University Press, 1963.

made by my father's
steel rods spraying orange,
yellow, red on a cold winter's
night after supper.

My mythic fire-maker
was not in a far off Olympus,
he was welding with acetylene
in the back yard.
Daddy, my Hephaestus.

## Ketchimaki's Farm

"From the eternal cottages of the Abode of the Dead."
—Runo 16, *The Kalevala*


When your cat disappears,
you are weeping in worry,
and your Dad says,
"Daisy is at Ketchimaki's Farm."
It's out there near North Lake,
a great place, where cats
live forever, playing and hunting."

When your dog disappears,
you are weeping in worry,
and your Dad says,
"Porky is at Ketchimaki's Farm.
It's out there near North Lake,
a great place, where dogs
live forever, tussling and napping."

When puppies and kittens disappear,
Your Dad says,
"The people at Ketchimaki's Farm
found homes for them.
A lot of the neighbors come to
take sauna on Saturday nights,
and Ketchimaki gives them a pet."

Picture it,
a U.P. farm, with a barn and sauna,
weathered gray wood, a lot of cats and dogs
scampering about having fun, never fighting,
plenty to eat, field mice and chipmunks,
and hay to sleep on when the snow
gets 10 foot high and the icicles grow long.

## Pinecone

> "Bring some cones from a fir,
> Some scales from a pinecone."
> —Runo 20, *The Kalevala*

When great emotion comes
the avoidance and pity
is a pine seed enfolded in cone
and dropped from the trembly
needles of a virgin white pine,
packed tight, brought by a
squirrel into a hole in a
dead tree pecked by woodpeckers
to white tan dust spread
upon the brown fallen
spines beneath,
and the worms
push downward, leave small
piles of composted renewal.

When it's time to freeze, it's
deep, like a chasm in Lake
Superior while it's lashed,
swept by wind to the
shore where it leaks into
the spore of a mushroom
smelling like shit, but beneath
and above like the whimsical
fronds of blown dandelions,
fallen from the fist
one flake at a time and
beginning, once again, to bloom.

Then, like the forked tongue
of adder or asp,
one is alone and sad, and
there lolls a thin shard

to belie the truth as clearly as a
blue sky high-pressure day clouded
over suddenly by a thunderstorm.

j a n e   p i i r t o

## Spectre on the Seney Stretch

> "The wolves made a rush there."
> —Runo 26, *The Kalevala*

1:30 A.M.
speed outruns the headlights,
eyes sweep right, left,
look for deer eyes
yellow in the glow.
Where there's one deer
there are more.

No other traffic.

In the distance
a big white dog
eating, bent over
in the road's center
of rising fog.

The head rises,
pointy ears,
the tail fluffy, long.
Brake, swerve
to the shoulder.
Maintain control.
Not a dog.

A wolf.
A white spectre
more ghost than canine.
Once, at a lecture,
the wildlife biologist
for the DNR
said he has never seen
a wolf in the wild.

Hmm. This creature is mine
and mine alone. No witnesses.

# jane piirto

## Iron Man

> "There bog-iron ore came to the surface
> and a steel ingot grew."
> —Runo 9, *The Kalevala*


Daddy was a welder, an iron worker.
Look at this house he built,
the metal, the iron, the sturdy.

On the backyard hill
the chain swing still swings that he built
when I was in 4th grade in 1951.

The top of the buried concrete bucket
still shows the initials, L. T., my classmate,
on whom I had a that-day crush.

He blasted the basement out of a solid ledge.
He dug it with a draft horse
in 1938, jacking up the house.

Water in spring dashes to the drain,
in the poured concrete slanted floor,
the only basement in our mining neighborhood.

He set the balcony deck like the swing
into barrels of concrete
with iron welded beams.

Flat heavy squared iron plates
strewn around the yard,
provided purchase on walls and fences.

When we sold the house in 2022
all was still solid, plumb, steely.
Iron lasts, even with rust.

**names**

Proudly Paavo presented
his copy, numbered as 1/ —
first in a fine new printing,
given with thanks for the work he'd done
for Finnish culture in Michigan:
*Kalevala*, in a case.
Deeply contented, his face
shone, silence hinting
of the joy one wishes men.

The story he told
of his own family's adopted name—
with Finland's freedom it came,
not so very old,
dropped the one Swedes forced on them,
contemned, opted for the same
of a runner of Olympic fame.
"Sisu" is a word all of his kids know,
useful up here, with the cold and snow.

His wife's ethnic stock's
maybe named for a small inland town
by a small lake (still enough to drown)
east of Vaasa, named for Swedish kings,
grew up inland here, south of the locks.
Identity clings to things any root brings,
then stories grow, like soil on the rocks:
A bear ate her pies, she said,
"but left the banana bread."

In Stockholm near half my friends were Finns.
Ilmari's name came from the *Kalevala*'s pages,
in a minting renewing the ages:
*Väinämöinen* a new time and place stages,
and all with what that word, "homeland," wins.

b. harlan deemer

As soon as I saw the view I said, "I'll buy." —very much aware
of many features that North and this North share.
My car guy's the scion of this town's founders, fishers from Sweden.
Have I now found my own one-acre Eden?

Jim's Ojibwe by his claim,
loves most machines, has a pontoon boat;
he bears a Swedish last name.
His grandkids can canoe; I took note—
he thinks Mackinac's great turtle story is just odd.
A Harley's his god,
a well-established Yooper with hindsight's frame.
With handy Jim's helping hand I planned
to add to my home and land.

The house in order,
no need to transition to "trooper,"
here I'm happy as a troll,
glad to embrace that label,
as long as friends laugh with me at table.
I wonder if that word's heard,
plays any real role
in the Upper's western third
along Wisconsin's border?

All these connections have mixed and matched.
We'll see how well I'm called to fit in, and how
called, maybe after I have died; for now,
like this land's many layered, rocky bands, patched,
my small part of a very large whole
takes heart, aims to find a good life's goal.
For what gain aims? I've not come for fish or farms,
not lumber, mines or quarries,
just good slumber, no alarms,
my new home's unnamed stories.

**half moon at twenty to noon**

The moon touched my skin.
I desired to let it in,
but it smiled, "Not yet."
"When the snow gets here,
the light is full aglow, the night, clear,
your heart's pull—regret,
then we'll be well met.
You will know how dear
are your shining years of debt
to life on Earth's sphere.
They may seem much less amiss,
your bets on love a near win,
you and I akin.
You may ask for just a kiss.

**a sleek, winter white sentence**

I can't be certain
Herman (its sex till undetermined)
liked my home. It came,
squirmed in somewhere yet unknown,
looked around, eyed me, down, up,
assessing how tame
I am, took the turkey thrown
near the plastic cup
of water it later tipped
on the tan tile floor.
Inquisitive, tight-lipped, guessed at suggestions,
two visits to date, no more,
all guests are questions
knocking on that sermoned door.

**ahead of wishful thinking**

This first day of fall
be all time ever to come,
summer in its stall,
small, gold leaves the sum
of change, though with today's dawn
thrummingbirds are gone,
and, along highways' lips,
orange tinges the trees' tips.
The bridge's towers—shadows
in the lake's thin haze
beyond my bay's low white caps' shallows
guide a tanker to the islands' maze.
Home anchors through seasons' shifts,
from stormy rancors and house-high drifts.

**stomach**

Now November starts
the long march to and through March
with ice pressing hearts,
naked as a larch,
Tamaracks taken to task
in the gut-grinding, care-crunching cold
finding life put half on hold,
bound in a scarf as a mask.
Feed the 2- and 4-footed fauna;
find comfort in beer, smoked meat, and a sauna.
Get through the drifts' double starch;
add fat, for survival's sake,
to your diet's intake 'til the lake
brings spring across the bridge's high arch.

**slowly rising temperatures**

A wide, white expanse,
this frozen bay's a blank face
except some scars' trace
where flesh took a chance
to cross: snowmobiles' brief race,
deer dared the free space,
and, far away, 3 crows dance.
Or maybe ravens.
Is this winter's peak?
What words enhance sights so bleak?
Where are thoughts' warming havens?
I have sought, and seek, Heaven's bright glance.
Until the lake springs a leak,
only Time's tense ticking song enchants.

b. harlan deemer

**nest**

Here, I hope, you're home,
wherever else that be true,
adhere when hearts hew.
Not all leads to Rome;
my graveled dirt road,
though travelled by few,
opens to a soothing view,
offers searching abode.
Eagles cross my bay, lure sight
to wonder where they may rest at night
by the lake's broad aerodrome.
Best were you would stay on through
each breath each day drew.

**Teach: Field Trip**

Second grade:
Mrs. Nelson letting us watch
the filmstrips rewind.
Little animated Hiawatha,
one of the good little Indians,
running,
fringed pants falling up,
the resolution into conflict as he ran backwards
out of the shelter of the forest canopy,
into the open field where the only way to hide
was to go down.

Twilight classroom of many shadows,
the children but outlines;
the only way I knew them was by their position in the rows.
Dismemberment of a resolution came
in flashes through the trees;
faces sparked and flared like match-heads
as the projector effused
a confetti drizzle.
The alphabet train above the screen assembled
itself into words;
tracks came into the liquid blue of my iris, splashed,
switchbacked on a mountain, peaking;
each lettered car was full of the chiseled alphabet
blocks that I played with at even younger years,
the ones I stacked into mountains that didn't amount
to any language,
then knocked down.

Echoed laughter steamed the engine—
the screen went blank—
settle came into the room.
The reel wound to the second spool
and the film tag slapped the projector—

chad faries

engines stopped.
It was over.
It was the beginning.

**Empire**

My empire is hollow and resonates among the Fall.
The doors are blown off our shops.
Photos of us in vintage litter the streets.

I give my steady strum and the leaves
of red that waif from broken limbs.

We smile and ache our teeth into whispers.
Cats come from the corners to warm our laps
while love notes pasted to the walls free
themselves and attach to the limbs.
We would start again like this
and keep touch close, tip level—
make trees anew.

Can we dance among the taxidermy
on Mahogany bars in the Upper Peninsula?
Name it for me: Pike's Bar. Pool balls
shocking the air we tread in gasps and giggles.
The Jukebox. Want is here and Willie Nelson.
Oh what I would do for a fish-fry and a close dance,
A cat nudging my hand.

I am with you in a cabin in a hundred
foreign countrysides. Meat is in the air.
Water from a brook is crisp and spills
from my lips as I go down
to love you at the perimeter,
our meaty metaphors of loins and breasts
manifest at the tip of my tongue.

Where are the choir boys singing of this,
Or the whores on Omuhundro St?

I will jump the Norfolk Western for you,

take it to the Elizabeth and swim past the sailors to the sea,
swim past the Outerbanks and flee.

Gather the blankets and cover me with triangles and xylophone notes.
Show me the corners and we will hide together while we float.

**Iron Family Vignettes**

### I. Faith Rodeo

Chipped church spires stab at the fat bellies of dust clouds kicked up from the hooves of painted horses heavy with plump, sequined princesses running incessant circles around barrels hustling for the right time; heathen kids ride ATVs wild down abandoned train tracks, dead ending at mine shafts, yawned open, screaming for a purpose.

### II. Northern Light

Horizon lifts the green from the tree line and swirls it into light straining through the colander of night. Punch drunk with love, we sit on a shore parting one another's bangs among a whorl of leaves on the nape of brush. A deer grooms a fox and a raccoon prunes a black bear. I fumble for words and silver snaps on blue denim trying to unravel the universe on the shimmer of a great lake.

### III. Grabbing Markers

How did I miss the colors of a peacock or the march of flower meadows across your journal pages? The thorns of daytime soaps and the obesity of winter, a scrawled calamity of opera. Her hand, hampered by shakes and chafed skin opens reluctantly, alien-like, artichoked. Her birdsong in her hand, Jazmine's melody shatters the pages, a candy wrapper confetti. She has eaten all of it. Hand open like the fenestra of an aperture letting in the light and an etymological clarity, classy and refined. A vibrato of Lifetime movies in the palm. She clenches. Bam.

### IV. Guys and Dolls

Show me a naked Barbie and I will show you the best love I never had, the light through the apple blossoms flashbulb. I close my eyes and tiny fires start my pistons. I am running with horses. And when the dust settles, and the spurs waning twinkle is just a glint in a last wink of sunset rays, we will still be looking for romantic love on pages so temporal, they lift off, just as our fathers did.

### V. Clean

Call in the snowmobile cavalry for help and fat clouds, silver with age and regret, to blanket the county with a white so clean that even the ore pits' collapsed and sunken bloodshot stoned and opioid witness eyes blink away the redness with involuntary flutters and look clearly to a cold heaven that unites us in an Upper Peninsula quest for warmth and awkward understanding. Our home is river flow clandestine under the ice.

## 9th Avenue Love Song and Run
*for Shaina*


Running up 9th avenue rhythm toward lost cricket
chirp. A buck's horn perforates the skin of a cloud
wisp and the sunset cracks and bleeds out
over Iron River and I lift my legs higher.

Chest is a jukebox full of old 45s
and my soundtrack is the roar of thick love
and Bass leave drums. The strings of November air
quiver and the tunes shoot in waves
at the faded wood doors of houses gone by.

The incline is great and the neighborhood is sparse.
In any other city neighborhood is dense and social,
but here forest ekes out walls; cars are heavy and misted
with the spray of hard salts and rust aches up from the ore
into the guts of engines. Not like any avenue, but like disparate
kisses over many years, one enough for 5 acres.

There is a darling and a painting behind
one of the doors, and another is crowded
with beer bottles to the ceiling and another,
alone and full of wait and stories.

Your curls of hair at the edge of space, cirrus wiped
across the page of lonesome river town, mines and holes
dug deep. Run. A bead of sweat like the dew at the lips
of flat flowers in black and white, and the fat snow
dizzies the asbestos siding; black birds dot
and doodle love letters over the snow covered roofs.

Alto stratus grazes the tips of bone branch growing
out of ore where 9th avenue ends and opens into a bowl
of salvaged eyes. Time slings. Two abandoned dog
houses at the rim of a pit, the openings black square

eyes into the soul of mining. I know all of her dances
and am learning the steps with every foot planted
as I climb at the threshold of a doorway again. Again.

Shine at the top of the hill where run begins and words end
before the story. The cricket. How can a leaving occur?
Bend it so it comes back around. We can't leave things
like this, at the top of a hill exhausted with deer fleeing
for salt licks at the ridges of dream treading over caving
grounds. This is where the guitar sounds are supposed
to start taking us to climax and fall nights with mist
tucked into pockets of rain. Two fingers at your temples
smoothing out the creases of Ottawa lake water.

This is what run brings, and leaves. A leaving:
What is it when a giggle substitutes for a kiss?
Your neck is vanilla and lavender, tiger lily tongue.
The smoke twists tonight, alone, a head on a pillow
and deer dreams of your eyes caught in the headlights.
Crickets shine and rub their legs raw. Run.

**Unscheduled Guest**

Winter slogs on. Chilly and grey as sorrow. I live alone now—a widow's lament, I suppose. As I gaze out the kitchen window, I see a doe has found the bird feeder by the woodshed. I tap the window and she pretends to startle. Her hunger is a demanding mistress—but there is no danger here. She prances a few steps away— sniffs the air, snorts and stomps her foot. She looks familiar and I wonder where her twin fawns have gone. I toast her with my honey-laden tea. We carry on.

lake-effect sky
a reprieve from lonely
heart light aglow

# ellen lord

**North Country Haiku**

### I

dusk light in August
sunflowers look west and bow
a grand finale

### II

moonless night, alone
this yearning to forge a star
wagon hitching time

### III

barren pine at dawn
sundial in a field of grain
timeless and windblown

### IV

stark winter shoreline
a shivering glissando
of ice song and shine

### V

we slow dance on ice
snowshoes slap the frozen lake
Michigan winter

**Ontonagon in Da Noonlight**

Finally, after another ruthless squall, my world is spring-breeze warm. Whiffs of wind riffle marsh grass as winter loses its grip on the day. I smile at the shape-shift of poofalus clouds as they slide along in syncopated scud.  How courageous these crocuses appear, a harbinger for legions of delightful daffodils. I rejoice as green spires slide up, moist and tender, to reach for the sun. And what of this soul-sequined meadow—festooned with sparkle under a wild northern sky. Ha!

after the storm
swoonful eyes on blue
Michigan spring

e l l e n   l o r d

## A Rain Poem

I remember rainy days at Shakey Lakes Park
how the raindrops puckered and pinged the lake.
Tributaries of rivulets cascaded down the window.
The Shack was open but no customers came.

I remember feeling disappointed as the storm ebbed
how sand on the beach was wet and puckered—
and how clean the air smelled, except kind of fishy—
how random campers emerged from tents and looked up.

I remember, years later, standing outside under warm rain—
my husband kissing me in a midnight deluge—and more
slow-twirling naked in that August rain. And I remember
the last weekend we spent together before he died

how we lay entwined, looking out into October's
grey, all-day-say-goodbye    rain.

**Lake Effect Sky**

snow drapes the trees
many bent to breaking
elusive inspiration
and always, the wind—

why is sadness so near
I'll have to ask the nightbird
when she enters my dreams
I get so weary of pleading
with the Hunger Moon—

blanket of hoarfrost
murmurations of starlings
save me from myself

**Snow Day (Again)**

Yesterday's sun was dialed to "low-glow."
and now, a tease of longerday light beckons
the dormant garden to shift and groan.

Tonight, Snow Moon winks her milky eye—
slinks beyond the tree line unencumbered
and somewhere, a nightbird sings.

Sometimes, it's such a relief
to be languid and dreamy, nestled
with books and cardamon tea.

I don't miss that garden at all
sultry summer's seductive mistress
with her drunken bees and outlaw weeds.

And yet, this yearning—

**Hometown**

Trout Creek was a boomtown for lumber barons in the early 1900s. Bars and churches swelling with the devoted. Now, most everyone is dead or gone. We own the ancestral home, honoring the long lineage of widows—preserving stories. Tribal lore. I like the empty church on the corner, went to summer bible school there as a kid. Just one year. Don't know how they let me attend or even why I wanted to go (me, a Catholic girl). Something about being with my best friend. She was a "Holy Roller." That sounded mysterious maybe even sinful (venial not mortal). I loved their arts and crafts, songs and laughter. No tedious genuflections. Now, someone maintains the building, perhaps that old couple next door, both stooped and shuffling but methodical. Grass is always mowed, the walk shoveled in winter. A bit of sparkle remains in the stain glass door. I peek through windows, see empty pews, empty altar—wooden Jesus silent on the cross. There is a "For Sale" sign on the lawn. Maybe I'll call, make an offer. Turn it into an art gallery or better yet, a meditation hall and shrine. A place for all the lapsed Irish Catholics who cleave to pagan rituals. Offer classes in moon howling, snipe hunting and chainsaw art. I'd hire a biker tattoo artist—request "God is Naked Love" inked in blue on my heart.

e l l e n   l o r d

## Porcupine Mountain High

Fireflies emanate light
as translucent wings search
for Eros on sultry nights.
I know a girl who glows

like a blue-flamed star.
As a runaway child she inhaled
rays of sunlight floating down
the Presque Isle River.

Now, luminescent—she sings
on the shores of Lake Superior
in a whirl of silky moonshine—
coyote serenades the night

and the eerie loon echoes
her primal song.

## Emily the Dōan's Text

*No zazen this morning.*
*The zendo got hit by*
*a skunk last night*
*and it was so*
*unbearable I had*
*to leave.*


Two miles down shore from the farmhouse
Lake Superior Zendo Aurora Dharma Temple
the message lit the bedside air blue
at 5:33. Sinking back I recalled running
the forest road after midnight, the luck
of one streetlight high in the pine boughs
so I saw movement, stopped. A mother
led her three kits across, everyone ready,
tails up. Now in the little parking lot
beside the Blue Link Party Store, a young couple
beside their black Jeep. She opens the cooler lid.
He drops the bag of ice on the asphalt
to break it up, tears open the plastic,
pours the ice rattling in. They turn out
onto Third, rooftop Kayaks snug in cool sunshine.
Natural Resources says the cougar moving
muscle-rippled shoulders across the meadow
in the field camera photo over by Ironwood
likely walked from South Dakota or Wyoming
in search of new territory. We give names
to places. Remake some unrecognizable.
Aim to turn the dharma wheel unceasingly.
Have mercy on us. We too belong
to the wilderness with all beings.

**Marquette Update**

Gather in, my ghosts. I've gone all over town searching for you.
Winter gray turnouts along the shore. Slow past former houses.

Old cemetery in the snow, obviously. The empty picnic pavilion,
cold-to-the-touch table where I looked across to islands and low mountains
as if into a time before sorrow. Lighthouse on the shipless horizon.

Today, for example, came an approaching constellation, young family
in coats and gloves and hats, all five with bright headlamps
though it was only fading afternoon. Only a park.

The bouncing, wandering, glowing points eclipsed their faces.

The father gathered snow from a bench, pitched the snowball
deliberately short of one of his little ones, a provocation answered
with a toss from a comically big, pink glove at the end of a short, bundled arm.

Maybe it's not so bad, being replaced. To watch others searchlight
their wintry way down shore and into the woods.

Another pine was half toppled beside the path to Sunset Point.
I remembered your music in the small waves below.
Ice-glazed boulders. The birches you knew.

Surrendering, I turned back toward my grocery list, over the bridge
at the mouth of the Dead, and saw four skaters with hockey sticks,
two little nets on the riverside pond. Gear bags, boots, and coats

dropped back on the snowed-over gravel boat ramp.

I walked snowed-over ice out to the rink they'd cleared, asked to watch,
to which the one wearing a helmet answered *sure!*
and they all skated and smacked the puck faster, harder.

The power plant's been decommissioned, by the way. Twin smokestacks

already down. Mastodon steel buildings abandoned to background
through bare trees on the bank between river and pond for the game.

So here we are. The last thin light of a late December afternoon.

The skate shush of boys younger than some of your deaths, suspended
on water where I've summoned you because I thought you should know.

j o n a t h a n   j o h n s o n

## Twenty-Five Miles from Milk

The piano in the pickup doesn't know
it's leaving loon song over dusk water,
the heron's glide, the duck's bank, and dragonfly.
The woman's childhood feet on warm dock planks.
Her parents' rare afternoon in the loft
alone, making her. The drowsy specks of flame
that rose into the stars, the moon, the Mars.
There's no indignity in the careful climb,
slow up the rutted drive cathedraled in pine.
The totter, jostle and jolt at the switch back,
the grip and gravel spit where it's always the worst,
where once, in snow, the dad broke an axle
gunning for the top, story of cables and a come-along.
*I'll show you the turtles!* but the piano
will play its rubato in town without the water-
wing-flap of a rising goose. Under stars
with silhouettes of pine, the log walls have long settled.
Twenty-five years the sawdust's gone from their hair.
The grandfather hasn't the heart to tell the trees
the new owner's rich and mean. Breathing alone
in town the town's changes, awaiting a tune, the piano
has no lyric for loving just one piece of land.

**Two Daughters**
*for John Howko*

Let's not pretend either one
grew up to like getting firewood.
Neither is sentimental like that,
though there's something about
a flannel shirt now and then,
something about how he tried every fall
to Tom Sawyer them into the adventure,
forest road jostle far into the forest,
riding the woodpile back where their seat
in the Blazer usually went, each load
to unload and make two circles
in the driveway, each around
a chopping block where he'd split—
back and forth—in the center of one
while from the other they'd collect
with their fuzzy gloves the quartered logs
smelling of maple grain and freshly blond
as the smaller one's curls were then,
until the last load, and here,
yes, after teasing him for his failure
to instill any romance for the Wood Chore,
they remember with him, for him,
late in the day, leaning atop the wood
for the turn into the Munising A&W
finally and what, even now, the taste
of a root beer float brings back.

jonathan johnson

## Process

I drive three days, row out
through headwinds and chop
over a ship wrecked to timbers
and into the mooring field,
scramble in the bobbing to grab
and tie off my wooden dory
to a vacant buoy, tuck in my oars,
settle back low in the hull,
open a pocket notebook, and float.
Ten dinghies crowd the hidden beach
beneath the maples behind me.
Summerun, Windsong, Thunder
and even Lickedy Spilt make
good company tugging their lines,
flag snap and halyards tinging
against their masts. How does
that passing duck manage
against the wavelets?
On shore, the town of my dead
is the town of my living who love me.
I can smell the wild roses this far.
Out here, seagulls ride the air.

**Samu as Cutting Wood a Winter Ahead**
—*early autumn, Alger County*

After the rain I promise myself just
one tank before a late dinner.

Sharpened chain sinks through lichen
and gray skin to open a cascade

of maple's hidden interior as blond
sawdust. The little poles go quickly.

The thick, dark trunks take a while,
down on one knee in the hot exhaust

and damp fiber smell as the saw bar
disappears. Steady growl and shush

of full throttle through earmuffs.
When the gap finally begins to close

at the top of a log, pull the bar clear
from the bottom. Never touch the ground.

The saw idles back, break locked,
resting on the stack of stove lengths.

A spider climbs from a deep bark fissure,
runs, and I remember this morning's zendo

*vow to save all beings* and lift this one's terrain
and set it down on the stack carefully.

Later, nearing the end of this log deck,
I start to wonder, each time

the throttle hesitates, if this is it—empty.
Then the engine growls and grabs again.

So it goes, not yet old but getting older.
Inside, someone I love is seasoning the steelhead.

I move faster. Cuts up. Cuts down.
Toss the lengths to either side,

cut again. Revving through rings
of all those standing seasons that made this tree,

I remember. Joy burns not by time or effort.
*Virtuous field far beyond form and emptiness.*

And with a few logs left, a faltering,
a surrender in the trigger. A sigh.

I pull my earmuffs off. The engine ticks.
Dusk. Into which an eagle somewhere

whistles a note, softer than one would expect,
above the house, the still water, the woods.

## John A. "Curley" Krainak
*March 13, 1915–September 4, 1986*

His skin was the pallor of late-night television.
His dirty painter's cap was perched above
his round wire glasses and bad teeth.
His neck jowls looked like turkey wattle.
His white hair had the grime of brown.
His trousers never spelled out his thin legs.
His black rubber boots stayed unfolded.

His garden consumed his entire backyard.
He smoked cheap cigars that dulled
the lilting wafts rising in the springs
of his garden blooming in puffs.
Each spring I waited not to smell him
as I peered deep into the razzle of flowers
unleashing fragrances abuzz with bees.

Summers later he came into our house.
He pointed to my ears, mumbled, and laughed.
I never understood a word he said
as he talked with my parents. All I grasped was
what drifted into the ears of my nose:
beautiful music profaned by a scratchy voice.
He chuckled when I pointed out his cigar stink.

Years later he died. His garden withered away.
New people have moved into his dark pink house.
The backyard is an unkempt mat of grass.
I can still see his ghost crouching there, his stink
rising from the dead past the rows of plants
he so loved into pure submission of color.
He was a tall trellis. I was just a silly weed.

**That One Time I Fell Asleep in the Garden Behind the Three-Stall Garage**

The soil, dank and dark,
seeped between my toes.

I couldn't stop wriggling.
The edges off the beaten path

were like cookie crumbs,
fresh and wet out of the oven.

Here and there were tiny nubs
of weed emboldened

by the bucketfuls of rain
a few hours before.

The kisses of sun
blanketed the shimmering

green tongues. I knew
I couldn't linger long.

I had every intention
of plucking those weeds

and shaking their white toes,
but I knelt before a bouquet

of green beans, hanging
full of muscle. Its skin felt

slightly hairy, firm. I glanced
over at the Lewinskis' house

and back at Mike's car
parked next to his house.

I snapped off a thick pod
and scrunched it in my mouth.

I tasted more than the earth.
With the sun exploded inside me,

I had to go lie down
as if I were buried

among the green cornstalks
standing guard over me.

I closed my eyes and inhaled
something richer than death,

more puzzling than the tart apples
that developed black moles,

more dazzling than the dragonflies
that pranced about the swamp

beyond the railroad tracks
careening near Montreal River,

the artery that led north into
the vast heart of Lake Superior,

where veiny waves throbbed
against the warmth of life itself.

As I practiced my dying,
I did not sink into the soil.

Instead I felt as if I was baked
into a cloud drifting away.

r a y m o n d   l u c z a k

## Chipmunk

*in English and American Sign Language (ASL) gloss*

<table>
<tr><td>

one bit me  
when I was five  
at Bay Cliff Health Camp  
I have no recollection  
of how I extended  
my finger  
even now  
years later  
their brown eyes  
still peer at me  
from the side  
asking if that family story  
about me  
was indeed true  

</td><td>

me age five  
happen  
B-a-y C-l-i-f-f Health Camp  
c-h-i-p-m-u-n-k {bite-my-finger}  
happen how  
{point-to-finger}  
{move-finger-to-chipmunk}  
not remember  
years later  
still {them} eyes brown  
{them-look-at-me-from-the-side}  
ask-one-ask-another  
family story relate-to-me  
true-biz happen ??  

</td></tr>
</table>

## Here Lies the Body of a Deaf Boy

Here lies the body of a deaf boy
covered with a linen sheet of white,
centered perfectly atop the oval table
aligned under a vast half-moon lamp
in the kitchen. He is sweating
under the hot glare, the babbling
among the people encircling the table.
He knows just what they want
from having observed him. Their eyes
keep demanding in so many words.
He really is too much of a hassle.
Those ears are a real problem.
They love him, as siblings should,
but really, who wants to repeat anything?
Secondhanded jokes are no fun.
Such a party pooper! They want him
to suture back into the blankness
of the sheet clothing the table,
seating the plates, glasses, and silverware.
He needs to disappear just enough
into their gluttony of food and laughter
so none of them has to feel guilty
when they do not hear him laugh like they do.
Everything is silent, sterile, safe.
What it cannot lipread will hurt no one.

r a y m o n d   l u c z a k

## Segueing

Remembering is how you get into the recording studio and stand inside a room with dots punctuating the corky walls and there's a music stand with sheets of music with em-dashes for where the lyrics are supposed to be but you don't know what you're supposed to sing so you hum whatever pops into your head and you start singing about that one time your mother took you downstairs to the JCPenney's one August and there was a pair of blue Nike shoes you really really really wanted because you had never seen such tapered sneakers before and it had this cool white swoosh on the side and your body was a huge sigh when you walked back and forth across the mirror angled from the floor and how cushiony your feet felt and how cool you were going to look on the first day of school all the while conveniently forgetting that you were never cool with these snotty hearing kids to begin with so you walk around and around and around until the world before you has no sharp demarcations between the spiffy shoes and your mother's eyes rolling and the dark gray industrial carpet and the pale yellow lights hanging above us in the basement and the rubber-sticky beige steps up to Aurora Street outside where the world of Friday nights and fish fry at taverns everywhere was starting to collapse into an armful of sprinkly lights and you would just bounce off the curb and onto the street before leaping so high into the heavens where along the way you would sprout wings and fly away so fast you'd never come back until years and years later when you are rich and famous but by then the JCPenney's no longer exists there so it's now a gym or is it a car dealership now but it really doesn't matter cause when it comes to memory there are no lines to cross either it is there or it isn't and what isn't is waiting to be found in the shoebox that you threw away once you got home and hopped on your bike because you were so excited to be wearing those new shoes and that's when you found your lost song all over again forty years later and your voice is soft as a peach with a heart of desiccated bitterness but the force of your words blows out until the entire downtown is the aftermath of a nuclear explosion with nothing left to remember and it's already September again

                                                      **yooper poetry**

## News Record Printing and Supply

The storefront had two glass-paned eyes
with a door for a nose. Inside
a harbor of docked office desks anchored
typewriters for sale. The store was
both a sea monster and cat biding its time
to ensnare any one of us kids
who dared slip into Hulstrom's next door,
the evil palace of penny candies,
comic books in rickety revolving stands,
and cellophaned pornographic magazines.

That one time I ventured into News Record,
its air was full of fog that I felt
weighing down on my shoulders.
I felt I needed a peabody jacket
to weather the storm inside
I didn't know was already brewing.
All those typewriters, and so expensive!
Was there anyone in the store? I vaguely recall
a faceless woman with cat-eyes.
Her posture whispered, *No trespassing*.

I didn't know how to type then.
I didn't have the know-how to measure
the weight of my thoughts into words.
All I wanted was a brand-new ship—no idea
how I'd navigate it—holding me steady
against the sickening waves of Lake Superior,
threatening to offer up my wind-thrashed body
to where the gods would turn me
into a monster like her, full of silences
clawing my bullies into tiny fillets.

raymond luczak

## My First History Teacher

Boy, how my hormones sang, and *sang*,
each time I walked into his classroom.
I could not believe a man's thick beard
could be so scintillatingly beautiful:
mostly black with slivers of rust brown.
His lefthandedness endeared me to him,
especially when he had to jot down a note,
as if reflecting my own awkwardness
like a mirror, only that he was far more
graceful than I ever would be at thirteen.
My swampy voice was overly nasal.
My freckled face was over-pimpled.
My body hearing aids jutted like flat breasts.
Even a few of my female classmates
tried to eyelid their aches from him.

There he stood, wearing a plaid shirt
inside a crew sweater and corduroys,
pontificating about historical incidents
and our next homework assignment.
He never knew how his smiles tortured me.
Even though he was married, I never-
theless wanted a place in his own
history. I didn't know that it was possible
for two men to fall in love with each other.
I hadn't quite understood just how small
my world was then in Ironwood.
I didn't know that there would be others
far more beautiful, and far more
accepting of me when I was older.
My future was not yet my history.

## Time of the Black Flies

*Brockway Mountain, Keweenaw of Michigan*

It took so long to get there because we stopped so many places on the way.
We climbed and climbed a muscled ridge that lay like the arm of a giant
almost in the middle of the Great Lake Superior, so blue and so cold,
and dangerous to swirls of hawks that soar back to where they were born,
which we came to see, when fifty feet below the cliff
a sparkle caught our eyes, almost hidden in the new shiny leaves
that just came out of the snow.

A piece of chrome bumper shot a ray of sun,
and made us point our binoculars down, instead of scanning the skies
on Brockway Mountain Drive. A car went over the cliff how many years ago?
A fifties model few remember anymore what cars looked like then,
and how it got there long forgotten. Was anyone in it when it plunged?
Branches grow through its windows—a little-known shrub called wild lilac.
Out of place from its home in the west, every year to bloom,
but hardly noticed when it flowers, because it's the time of the black flies,
and nobody wants to stop and look too long.

Only a little like a lilac, the bundles of tiny flowers more pink than purple.
A cluster that fits the look of a lilac close enough,
so instead of *Ceanothus* people call it lilac.
A flower we only acknowledge in spring. Anywhere you stop and look
along the Mountain Drive you'll find that rare, red-stemmed shrub,
as the hawks glide oblivious above this finger
in a lake you can see on a satellite photo.

The view forever in all directions, at a spot with no guard rail,
amid the lime-green leaves and youthful rush of spring—
the mystery of birds, the flora, and the car over Brockway.

dana richter

## A Mushroom Is a Microscopic Kind of Thing

The toadstool on the forest floor
Is nourished by a tiny thread,
A microscopic tube,
Digesting as it goes,
Oozing gluey juices,
In wood or straw it grows.

Incessantly the dead it seeks,
Meekly, silent and in secret,
All the while never sleeping,
Even insect bodies reeking
Satisfy its micro-soul,
Its quiet need for breeding
In sweet odiferous decay.

So when we see the mushroom,
Its unseen work is done.
No longer shy but wallowing
In its mushy success
The sodden filaments gather
To make a fleshy organ
Rising in unabashed reproduction.

The wondrous fruiting body,
Sinister but beautiful,
Innumerable forms—
Stalk and gills and teeth and pores—
Sending billions of spores,
Floating back safely
To the invisible world.

## Rutabaga!

*—a vegetable that deserves the status of a fruit.*

Rutabaga! Rutabaga!
There couldn't be a better bag'a
Edible roots for the table!

A cole of great proportions,
Sprung from the lowly mustard,
Whose root got out of control!

Royal purple tops or Swede turnips,
No matter the name they're given,
They're the Garden Goddess blessing,
To satisfy a simple person's palate,
For what would be a pasty,
Without big chunks of rutabaga?

Root, root for the rutabaga!
Just some seed is all you need—
"They grow themselves," the packets say,
Never mind your desires.

Rutabagas grow slow confined to rows,
So let them out and let them roam.
Scatter them in spring—or anytime!
Pluck them young like radishes,
They're sweeter and more tender,
And steamed rutabaga greens
Will give you health forever!

A biennial, to make more seed,
You must not dig them all in fall;

The ones you leave will sprout in spring,
Several shoots from a single crown,
Living off the over-wintered juices in the root;
Giving birth to yellow blossoms,
Whose petals, in crucifer fashion,
Grace the garden all summer long,
For you to nibble while hoeing,
Or to add a bit of bite to your salad.

*Brassica napobrassica* is the rutabaga.
Perfected by the Scandinavian taste,
Brought from Central Asia,
Norsemen survived on rutabagas,
Filling the holds of their ships
With the fat roots on long trips,
Discovering new lands
Where to grow more rutabagas!

And when the rutabaga reached Finland
It met its greatest love,
And was born the phrase,
"Happy as a Finn in a field of rutabagas."

The most cherished moment though
Will come in the cold, calm,
wet air of spring,
As you till the new garden soil,
And strike a buried treasure.
Then, the fragrance of rutabaga arises,
Its sweetness, its pungency surrounds you,
Like the breath of earth herself,
Tempting of rutabaga. —ahhhh ...

## Mushrooms in the Huron Mountains

When the September rains have come
Mushrooms would pile high the tables
In the Stone House on Ive's Lake in the Huron Mountains,
The summer home of John Longyear,
Who made his fortune on land, logs and iron-ore
From the U.P. to Minnesota,
And started the Huron Mountains Hunting and Fishing Club,
With a dozen other rich barons from Marquette, Chicago and Detroit,
At the turn of the century.

Sorted in groups by colors and types,
Mushrooms yet to be named by science,
On pages in obscure journals few will ever see.
Measuring their gills, their pores, their stems, their caps;
Recording astounding numbers of things called fruiting bodies;
In good years one could not walk in the towering forests of pine and hemlock
Without stepping on mushrooms.

While I lay sleeping in the creaking upstairs, the air thick with spores.
Once, while dreaming, when the moon had just passed full
And the rain dripped loudly on the tin of the porch roof,
I thought I felt something touch at the foot of the bed,
Like the brush of someone passing by.
Did someone come up the stairs I did not hear because of the rain?

Some say the house is haunted—they wouldn't spend a night there!
Maybe it was John Longyear himself roaming the halls—
His ashes were spread below in the lake he loved.
Or it could have been his son, who took his last canoe trip from Marquette
One fine June day but never got to the Stone House.
His mother, so fraught by the loss, no longer could live in that house,
Moved back to Boston never to return to her husband's paradise.

I always said it was the mice I heard, and maybe it was not a touch at all.
In morning I would examine the prints of spores
And study the mushrooms again, then go to the woods to get more.

**The Warbling Vireo**

It is the mother who sings
Sweet warbles all day,
Sitting on her nest,
Looking just like a leaf,
So well-concealed is she,
Afraid not the least to be seen,
By blue jay or snake.
While warming her eggs
She announces her joy of spring!
"Where am I? Where am I?"
Stand back and search—
But you'll never find her.
The tree itself is singing!

**Any Wayside Place**

Here is a soft nest of grass
dry in the late summer sun
that sits lower in the sky,
where I rest awhile
in view of wild apple trees.
Where spring petals once fell,
a few fruits have fallen,
for me to test their ripeness—
the ones on the tree still hard.
Other animals have already been here.

Goldenrods are way past prime—
only the tiniest yellow remains.
The weedy fields dotted with purple—
asters amid the frosted bracken ferns,
that always brown first,
now on the verge of decay.
Having spent another year dark green,
the maples in the distance
won't let summer go.

This old farm waste ground
once grew potatoes, oats, and hay,
now a multitude of weeds
that came with immigrants.
Thistle, yarrow, clover—
flowers admirable in their own way,
and wild carrot,
graced with the name Queen-Anne's lace.

A blue-jays shrieks
not a song but a warning:
"Danger! Danger! He's here! He's here!"
A raven croaks from a distant perch—
his turn to guard these fields and woods

from a line of sentries
across centuries.

Nothing is left to achieve
this time of year,
summer being mostly memories.
The first frost has already come
but the white in the morning
was barely noticed,
only the evidence the next afternoon.
Goals dreamed go unfulfilled.
This heart beats incessantly
to live and let time pass.
I slowly rise and walk ahead,
and lift an apple from the grass.
Sweet enough.
All I could want is here.

**Sorcery**

the creek pours over itself
folds the pregnant moon
into frothing corners of its mouth
the firefox spins in the yard igniting
auroras in the grass

I wander out
through the sparks, beneath
the chartreuse curtain of sky
a baptism
a cleansing

burn off the dross
of sick days, stalk
this stand of birch and pine with real feet
stumbling, real feet
falling over underbrush,
young wings blossom into flapping,
an owl in the dark

you wrap around me
masquerading
as a shield of stars,
seduce me over this edge where thirsty
root meets supple
bank and moonwater melds our skin
into something silver-smooth
and daring

the forest quakes
with sorcery and still,
no thing knows

except the moth
who is awake
eating light

**Reverie**


nightly
when the train barrels down the tracks and the mournful whistle blows,
coyotes come calling

they howl some primal lament my bones know
but the rest of me has forgotten
curse of descendants abandoned by progress
and white man's paintings
of Christ

they ride the night air
dance among clouds stained black
proclaim to loon-sung lakes the secrets of All Time
spinning fast
still as rabbit in her burrow

**Passion**

somewhere in the forest
a cherry bursts
between my teeth          juice drips
down naked chins and necks
down breasts and jawlines
pools
in navels
bare toes in supple soil
rocks both round and sharp
pits of cherries spat
as offerings for forest goddesses
and the Gods and vultures
of past unrequited wailings
*"More!"*
*"More!"* I cry.

Ferns sprout exuberant and tall
berries overgrowing
sweet ferns overgrowing
tickling soft-prickly
grasses cradle waxing sweat
of bodies crowding pale thighs,
hot and ginger
to the touch
and in the sky
maple leaves caress each other's thin-veined skin
while the wind stokes and sighs, kisses
folds of green and pink blushing,
wake the dawn in raven's mouths
as the hermit thrush braids its lust libretto from tree to tree
and a fox licks its lips from the bushes.

the river to the east hears no song
but the bewitchment in your eyes
blue and moonswept
whose language   is the same.

# jennifer elen bríd

**The North Shore**


Light-Bringer,

dance me to the edge
of lunacy

this highest tide
the perfect edges
of your lips rushing

seafoam silk
and never-full

these flowers fed by
roaring sea

the ones that wake
and weep in me

bloom

**Sweetness, Shared**

my second-favorite thing in the world today
is this maple leaf
the size of my face, gleaming candy apple
red with dappled
green, like a child streaked
it splotchy
in Granny Smith's kitchen

I can

taste it

sugar-hot and cinnamon
orchard's tang beneath a smattering
of honey-gold leaf mold                    and toffee,
how it hides
our lips pressed together
sweet and sticky

from the ravens
and the crows
the mountain ash
and nymphs
who are always tattling
to the sky

# jennifer elen bríd

**January**

my snowshoeing
has rustled up a
Great Horned Owl

her call

    hangs

like woodsmoke

drifting
      through
  to
  bone

## Sap Season

*in loving memory of Helen Haskell Remien*

everything is in a circle
they said
roundness of birch trees
bark thin and curling
Golden Lake,
the tires of the bike
that could have killed
me on James Lake Road
across from the sixteen acres where we tapped
maples for amber elixir,
stirring, stirring
in the cook pan sweet steam
and woodsmoke, a benediction
in that garage of logs and chipped chinking
snow-melt streaked
across the floor

some March not long ago
my friend Helen offered me
a jar of sugar water
the first of sap gathered
filled with Faery glee, her
body thin and curling

I had forgotten sap's mellow sweetness
how it courses through the body
how it made me feel at one
with trees

only the maples knew
or the Faeries maybe
that this would be her parting gift

# jennifer elen bríd

this woman made of leaves and honey
body housing nymphs and elves
wildflowers sprouting
from her lips

a song from my childhood
a verse I had forgotten

I think
that spring
the maples
wept.

## Come Like a Thief

*For Roger Magnuson*

Book of Revelation 3:3 ... If you will not wake up, I will come like a thief, and you will not know at what hour I will come [for] you ...

Answering his cry, I went into Roger's room, readjusting his pillow, his covers, cooing, "It's OK, it's OK." He fell back asleep. I sat at his bedside.

Out the window, my brother Albert stood on the sidewalk. Albert, who died of melanoma, stood there as Lake Superior pummeled the shore, and maple leaves, tongues of fire, fell from a blue, blue sky. Stood there in three dimensions, age 17, I'd say, in jeans and red flannel. Then I saw him hit a four bagger over the bleachers, spear a pass from the quarterback, heave to the finish line, long before tumors covered his body, before he lay under an oxygen tent, before he forbade me to name my son Albert: "Don't do it," he warned, "It's a bad-luck name." A photo of Great Uncle Albert, knickers and high tops, flashed before me, Great Uncle Albert who died of tuberculosis at 19.

Hands in his pockets, my brother stood, looking right at me, waiting. Did he come to say it wouldn't be long? Did he come for Roger, or did he come for me?

**First Snow at Sunrise**


### 1.

This morning, I call my friend on the phone, wish her a sixtieth Happy Birthday. "I've forgiven Daddy," she blurts. I'm aghast. I'd punch him in the face, kick him in the groin, I think to myself. At that moment, my friend, with fervor of a saint, humbles me. I feel inadequate, question my ability to forgive. As we talk, assays and triumphs flicker before me, like cuts from film in a dark theater.


### 2.

Waves of the Pacific Ocean crashed and fanned across midnight sand on Stinson Beach, fracturing bits of moonlight. My friend sat beside me, alert, tense as an anxious doe, took in the smell of seaweed, she did not like, unable to let the ebb and flow of ocean soothe her. She picked at dune grass, her breaths deep, filled with her childhood. A group of tourists on the crowded beach jogged by too closely. She recoiled, shifted toward me as waves continued to splinter the night.


### 3.

We sat on the shore of Lake Superior, lighthouse in the distance, loon calling. "I couldn't remember what Daddy did to me when I was 12," she explained, "how he didn't hold back." I called to mind the hulk of her father, bit my lip to keep from crying, to give her full rein for telling. "With the help of my college counselor," she continued, "I'm piecing together the fragments of my busted self. Look at me, I'm in graduate school!" Look at me, I'm a project leader!" Soon came humility, empathy for others.

4.

Today, herself a counselor, my friend steadies young ones who travel roiling waters, guides them to safe harbor.

5.

Just as we are about to hang up, she holds her breath: "Oh, the sunrise!" she gasps. Fire and first snow fill her body with hope.

**The Vision of Eziel**

Luke 2:35 … And a sword shall pierce your heart.

## 1.

Eziel falls into a coma. The Virgin Mary appears and dresses her in a white robe. She whispers in her ear … Eziel is to found a chapel in honor of the Virgin at the highest point in the attic of her Victorian home. Fully Gothic, its cathedral ceiling will assure the upward gaze of eyes.

That evening, Christ descends, joins His Mother at Eziel's bedside, blood glistening from His wounds. Eziel drinks from the gash in His side. Christ slides a band onto her finger. When dawn filters through summer lace, Blessed Mother and Son ascend, seraphim chanting, the scent of roses filling the room.

## 2.

Eziel stops eating meat, takes mostly broth and kale she grows at her bay window, wears coarse burlap beneath her garments. In winter, she snowshoes in bare feet, from ache to exquisite agony, loss of the senses. *Durée*! Oh, ecstasy!

Before long, Eziel hires an auctioneer. Quickly goes her oak bed, its sturdy hand-carved posts and headboard; her tall armoire; the Bombay chest, its floral inlay and marble top. Equally goes the fainting couch, Limoges china, Lunt silver. Soon, she has all she needs for the chapel.

## 3.

In Christmas season, the bishop schedules an appointment with Eziel. He wants to see for himself that woman, that place. On his way, he thinks of her addled mind, her foolish claim that the Virgin has appeared to her, multiple times, in a grotto of chandeliers.

When Eziel opens her wrought iron door, the perfume of Madonna lilies fills the hall. Intoxicated by the scent, beauty and purity of the woman, the bishop loses his composure, falls into plush folds of a Louis XVI couch not yet liquidated. He bangs his head on its frame of fruit wood from France, probably pear.

Soon, the bishop takes his leave. He sinks into the seat of his car, clings to his steering wheel, sobbing. Beads of sweat form on his brow. His heart beats wildly. Finally, he quiets, collects himself but unsettles again, for before him, at the foot of an arbor, blue clematis pushes up from the snow.

4.

Eziel hires a carpenter. For the chapel, he builds a large Gothic arch. He carves bas-reliefs of *fleur de lys*, acanthus leaves, liana. At Butler Antique Mall, she finds a stained-glass window. In its lower panel, a pelican feeds her three young. Beaks having punctured her tender abdomen, they draw blood. Drops, big and swollen, fall from her wounds.

Eziel places the stained glass before two vertical windows at the back of the chapel. To the left, she stands her large statue of the Virgin clad in white gown, blue cloak, slender girdle at her small breasts. Light filters through stained glass, royal blue and red. Prisms play over the lips of the Virgin.

5.

Across the Upper Peninsula, from Copper Harbor to Whitefish Point to Sault Ste. Marie, from Big Bay to Marquette to Ishpeming, believers and non-believers come to the chapel, inspired by rumor or fervor. In light of votives and stained glass, amidst the scent of wild rose and hardwood maple, crystal Rosaries fracture light.

Women of Italian descent come, of Cornish descent, of Irish origin, of Greek origin, come. Ojibwa of Catholic persuasion, and not, come. Lutheran women— from the Finnish church, the Norwegian church, the Swedish church—also come to the Virgin. Jews come. Muslims come. Shamans, priests, pastors come. Rabbis, imams come. They petition for the safe return of daughters, of sons, of spouses, serving or captured, in Afghanistan, Iran, Iraq. In Jordan, Egypt, Libya. In Tunisia, Yemen.

6.

Since the opening of Our Lady's Chapel, scores have come home from military tours, from embassies, haunted by visions of entranced freedom fighters, mothers raped and killed, infants crying for them. Etched in memories forever is the blood of innumerable bodies, sacrifice that will resurrect cities, harvest wheat for bread, tap waters sweet as wine. In the chapel, revelations rain down. Prayer and weeping fill the evening, the night.

7.

Since the dedication of the chapel, Eziel has written a thousand psalms in honor of the Virgin, a thousand villanelles, in her honor, five hundred pantoums, scores of sonnets, ghazals, haiku, and more, all in her honor. Hundreds the Virgin has cured of heart disease, nervous disorders, depression ...

8.

At age 99, Eziel dies peacefully in her sleep. At her autopsy, the pathologist notes the uncommon swell of her heart, the way it fills her chest cavity, how, when he cuts it, blood falls in swollen drops.

## 9.

The funeral takes place at St. John's in Ishpeming in May. When the priest sprinkles holy water on Eziel's coffin, a strange sound, almost inaudible, emanates from within. Unnerved, the priest raises his voice. The heart persists. A sigh. A wave. Drumbeat in the distance.

## 10.

When pallbearers lower the coffin into earth, sun emerges from gray clouds, with blinding brilliance. Lilies of the Valley reach from Eziel's heart, through satin, through the bronze of her casket. Lilies of the Valley spring from soil at her grave, spill into streets of the town, across cities, across seas, atop mountains, into deserts. Everywhere, Lilies of the Valley bloom. Lilies of the Valley bloom. Lilies bloom.

**Resurrection**

> After Curtis Dawkins's painting *Whatever You Want It to Be* in the exhibition "Voices & Art Unlocked," featuring poems by members of the Marquette Poets Circle.

In her sitting room in Marquette, my friend Militza, now 94, listens to poems I read in French, about my significant other, recently departed.

Moved, she leads me to her library, reaches for a volume, red spine embossed in gold, the complete works of Jean Racine, seventeenth-century tragedian I studied when I lived and breathed French theater. "I can't take it with me," she says, dropping it into my arms.

Later, eyes tearing, I carry the tome to the trunk of my car, recall the urgent polish of Racine's alexandrines, caesurae, rhymes, my fear as his plot closes in, like Fate herself, when Phaedra reveals her desire for stepson Hippolytus, her husband away consulting oracles.

When Theseus returns, Phaedra lies to him, calls his son perfidious, calls him seducer. Hippolytus, horrified, almost murders her, drops his sword, flees to woods, to seashore, where mammoth bull rises from angry waters. Sparagmos, Sparagmos, call him Sparagmos! He spooks Hippolytus's horses, Hippolytus tangled, Hippolytus dragged, trampled, sliced on rock, unlimbed.

Might the bandage in the sky in this painting signify a wound, a false accusation that can never be undone, the injustice of it aching forever in the incarcerated person's gut? Or might the larva in center connote an unexpected drift toward optimism in court proceedings on his behalf? Like Hippolytus, whose innocence Phaedra discloses before committing suicide, his good name restored, the prisoner, broken Jesus body, emerges, lily intact and glowing on Easter morning.

## Bigfoot and Jim Harrison Skinny Dip in Morgan Pond on Father's Day

*for Kathleen H.*

They look like father and son as they wade into the shallows, Bigfoot three feet taller than Harrison and smelling like bear scat. Harrison smells of Dewar's and onion, and the crescents of his buttocks glow in the dusk like swans. The clay sucks at their shins as they move deeper, shadows of perch and rainbow darting away in startled splash and foam. Bigfoot keeps his eyes on Harrison, who has already fallen once on shore, tripping as he shed his pants and underwear. Bigfoot lays a hairy arm across Harrison's shoulders, leaves it there the way a moose might shelter a calf under its haunches during a thunderstorm. Harrison listens to the peepers drill the night with music, and he starts to hum, then sings, "And the cat's in the cradle and the silver spoon." He holds onto the last word, draws it out like a wolf howl. Bigfoot pushes his thick tongue to the roof of his mouth and coughs like a coyote in duet. Harrison is up to his nipples in water now, and he raises his one good eye to Bigfoot and croons, "Little boy blue and the man in the moon." His voice is full of booze and cigarettes, like logs in a flood. Bigfoot can't help himself, reaches down and scoops the writer up like a baby, rocks him back and forth, back and forth. Bigfoot knows the hunger of loss, has chased it through canyon and forest until the trees of his legs were weak as saplings. Harrison presses his head against Bigfoot's chest and sobs.

m a r t i n   a c h a t z

**Bigfoot's New Year's Resolutions**

he wants to gain weight
stand in the middle of woods
be mistaken for a landslide

he wants to exercise less
find a pine stump, sit on it
until his muscles turn to clay

he wants to eat more meat
every day find something furred, young
gnash, rip, floss his teeth with its skin

he wants to drink more
fill a creek bed with apples
swim and gulp the sweet rot

he wants more clutter
an old couch from the dump
newspapers that smell like perch

he wants to care less
piss in the mouth of the Chocolay
shit on the beach, not bury it

he wants to travel less
remain in his cedared cave
read long chapters of winter, sleep

he wants less time with his wife
let her take their cubs and leave
spend days gobbling silence like honey

he wants to procrastinate more
wake in afternoon sun, not hunt
until owls dissect the moon

## Bigfoot Meets a Homeless Man on Presque Isle

The man smells wild,
the way a black bear smells
after winter sleep, full
of hunger, dizzy from
root and dark. Bigfoot can taste
loneliness on the man, a sweaty
slick of days spent near
the big water, hidden in pine,
rooting through garbage cans
for leftover French fries, brown
apple cores still sweet and seeded,
hot dog buns gone chlorophyll green.
       Bigfoot knows
this man will die soon,
has seen it before when moose
with brain worm stumble off
by themselves, or one eaglet shreds
a feebler eaglet to get
more perch and salmon from
their mother's beak. Even this close
to lights and cars and houses, survival
is all about being bigger, stronger,
hairier, scaling trees for nested
eggs, scooping silvery spottails from Superior
surf, tearing haunches off mewling fawns.
       Bigfoot wants
to help the man who has wandered
onto this rocky thumb surrounded by wave.
Wants him to feel wanted
as soft leaves or a run of smelt.
As the man beds down for the night
under a ribcage of branches, Bigfoot
knuckles one tree trunk, knocks, knuckles
again, knocks. He does this until
he hears hollow, then scratch, chatter.

He plunges his hand into the tree,
extracts a panicked squirrel. Bigfoot snaps
its neck like a cricket leg. Holds
the carcass to his chest, breathes the last
pulses of its pebble heart, then grunts
an ape prayer of thanks, a sound
like a mother giving birth under
a blazing comet to something
necessary. Needed.
       Bigfoot leaves
the squirrel at the man's sleeping
feet, where he'll find it in morning
light. An offering of meat, blood, fur.
To remind the man that the world
loves him.

**Crossing the Straits**

It used to be harder, crossing
the Straits, like wagon training
through the Donner Pass or fleeing
Okie dust blizzards for the fruit
fields of California. My dad told
me about caravans of trucks, vans,
cars four hours deep on U. S. 41
in November, inching, inching
toward the sheet metal waves.
He would listen to Hank Williams
yodel on the radio, gobble ham
sandwiches with bread dark
as the backs of bears, coffee
blacker than a lunar eclipse.
All for that moment
when he rolled onto the boat,
paid the ferryman, and sailed
over those cold waters
to that place where even
the air smelled wild. Yes,
it used to be harder
to get to places you wanted
to go. From here to there.
Where deer come out of pines
to greet you, snow falls
like first or last breaths,
and the world is still
fighting to survive.

**Moose**

They are all around, like pine
needles or bracken or field
mice, but I have never
seen one with its building
of body, crown of branches.
They hide-and-seek with me,
staying deep in the forest
where the green heart of the world
beats. I've heard they walk
along lake bottoms, submerged,
holding the oxygen in their
lungs like buried treasure. That
is what I want. To see one
climbing from the surf
of Lake Superior, shaking off
water in great sheets,
gulping the fresh air. Like something
newborn, fresh from the womb
of God.

**Portrait of the Virgin Mary as Skunk**

She shambles, slow as a mud puddle,
bright arm of lightning splitting
the night of her body, peacock
plume tail sweeping the ground
behind her, the way, I imagine,
Mary swept sawdust from her floors
after Joseph was done for the day.

And think of that smell, part terror,
part warning. Mary calling
her son to supper, him ignoring her,
turning stones into toads, leaves
into salamanders. When he didn't
answer, Mary unleashed her quiet
wrath until it settled on his godly
skin, pickled him in maternal love.

## Doe After a Blizzard

My son noticed her first, splayed, bloody, broken by a neighbor's fence.

A dead doe, shining in the sunlight that always comes after a blizzard,

sunlight so strong it hurts to step into it. Sunlight that shouts.

The doe was haloed in that light, and my son, only five, said,

*Fix it, daddy*, reduced me to an Easter Island moai, stone face

immutable in the presence of suffering. I wanted to tell my son

*I can't* or *She's gone* or *She's with God* or some other

emptiness recited in church every Sunday so often that it has lost

its ability to comfort. Instead, I picked my son up, carried him

closer to the doe, whispered in his ear *Isn't she beautiful?*

I watched his face change, confusion give way to something

seraphic. *Yes*, he said, nodding. *Yes, she is. Yes. Yes. Yes. Yes.*

untitled

deer season opening day
pasties poker leinenkugal farts
venison hanging in garage


mosquito blackfly seasons
upper peninsula insurance policy
keeping civilization away


alone in wilderness beauty
god far from other people
staring in my face

**god's country**

finnish pasty fest
thimbleberry jam
brook trout beauty
hum of mosquitoes
winter venison stew
shot and beer chaser
lions and packer game
small town tavern
country-western music
playing on jukebox

**memories**

during season of long white
village seniors dreaming
of warm florida sunshine
forgetting when young
making snow angels
playing fox and geese

**yooper obituary**

waino knuttila
born in felch
dropped out of school
working family farm
years as a miner
sailing great lakes ships
cutting lumber in forest
began writing poetry
after retirement years
called "sisu bard"
loved trout fishing
annual deer camp
enjoyed going casino
warm summer naps
making wood
during autumn season
memorial service
calvary cemetery

**keweenaw reflections**

mines were abandoned
copper mining stopped
stamping mills closed
smelter whistle silent
gray cold smokestacks
casting dark shadows
scarred by lightning
train depot empty
tracks and crossties gone
rails going no where
engines rusting museum pieces
copper wealth vanished
reason for economic collapse
greed of company investors
labor union demands
too expensive to mine
copper ore simply gone
main street stores closed
churches stopped services
bar businesses booming
in mining row houses
mothers reading bibles
fathers lost in brown bottle ethers
dreaming of mines opening
going off welfare
working underground again
kids graduating from school
without local jobs
taking diplomas to
detroit milwaukee minneapolis
finding steady employment
with regular paychecks
only coming back
for home coming
school class reunions

most remaining businesses
relying on summer tourist trade
working hard three months
to survive rest of the year
when small towns and villages
enjoying quiet out of season
dreaming better next year

of water


stormy lake superior waves
leaving seamen's ghosts temporally on shore
before returning in receding tides


sun casting haze over lake surface
mysterious shadows rising in morning mist
wilderness ghosts vanishing in forest

**yooper samizdat**

attaching poems to trees
later like autumn leaves blown in wind
words scattered all over the world

**In Search of the Giant Killer**


As children
We roamed the meadow-covered hills
(with enough saplings to grab the leaves off the top of )
Parallel ridges and gullies stretching
Up from Lake Linden to Calumet.

Snow covered slopes in winter
Climbing up, saucering down
Sometimes flipping over
But never hurt
Only buried in soft fluff

One hill—the Giant Killer we called it
So big, so steep, so scary
So hard to stay upright
Perched at the top
Don't look down
Hold breath
Shove off into the void
Stomach flips, flops
Saucer stays upright!
Breathe
Exhilarating triumph!

Fast forward sixty-plus years
Walking old "first track" with grandchildren
Telling stories.
"I want to show you the Giant Killer."
But everything is different
Tall trees cover what was meadow
All the hills look alike
"There's the frog pond. It's not far now.
But was it one or two ridges after the pond?
No, not that one. It was bigger."

But where?
I never found it.

## Night Sky

Tiny sparks of light against black velvet
Infinite in time and distance.
As a child, I saw Orion in all his glory:
Belt and scabbard, raised arm on shield,
High above my frosted breath on the outdoor rink
Swirling around on my skates.

On my back on a cushion on the dock,
In August, Milky River flowing across the sky,
I count "falling stars" gone in a blink.
Sometimes not stars, but green curtains
Hanging, tempting me to reach out
To what I cannot touch.

Years spent with a night sky
So light polluted I could only see
The faint corner stars of Orion,
Or perhaps Venus early in the predawn cool
Of suburban Houston skies
As I walked, wishing to be back up north.

But then I wonder:
Is a cell in my body simply another
Night sky to someone in an inner micro universe?
And are the stars and galaxies I see
On Orion's belt or in that Milky River
Part of a skin cell of a giant living thing?

**Sounds While Sitting in Silence**

Inside:
Huummmm of the refrigerator
Puffffff of the gas log going on
Thut of the gas log turning off
Followed by the whirr of the fan sending out warm air
Tuc of the second hand on the clock

Outside:
Jeep, jeep of a distant bird
Chirp, chirp of another
Tap slap of a neighbor's screen door closing
Buzz of Ruby-throated hummingbird
Distant motor grinding
Wing flutters
Chatter of squirrels
And an annoying ORV shattering the peace
Of my Sunday afternoon

## The Crocus Race

*In fond memory of my mother, Celia Pearce Olson,*
*and her friend, Lucille Kolb*


"You know," she said to her friend from up the hill,
"Lake Linden sees spring before Calumet."
True, to a point.
The spine of the Keweenaw protects the valley village
From the worst of the northwest winds.
But, cold settles in the valley on calm days,
Sending the mercury huddling into a ball below the zero mark.
Who was right would be proved
When one presented the other with the first blooming crocus.

In a corner of her garden, between the kitchen window
And the living room bay, facing south,
Catching more rays than any other spot,
The first place to reveal garden dirt when melting began,
Well fertilized by birds feasting at the feeder
Attached to her kitchen window,
Hopeful spikes of life protruded from the dirty snow.
She would win the race.

"I told you so," she said when she handed her friend
A purple flower with sunny yellow stamens.
She won the next year, and the next, until …
Her friend filled a pot with dirt and crocus bulbs,
Placed it in her sunny south window
Right above the steam radiator
In January.
Watered, coaxed, coddled, covered it on the coldest nights.

In a blizzard near the end of February,
Her friend drove down the hill,
Rang her doorbell, held out the pot
Of purple blooms with sunny yellow stamens.
"I win this year!"

deborah k. frontiera

They laughed, clinked their teacups together,
Toasting the winner of the last crocus race.

**Leaving Home**

There was a time when all
I wanted was to leave
The town that made me what
I am to find my self.

Wanting adventure, anywhere
See the world out there,
And find my place in it.
As years went by, I found

My place, my heart, was back
Home all along. I never
Really left. My heart, my roots
Were always where I came from.

**Martin Achatz** grew up and lives with his family in Ishpeming, Michigan. He holds a Master's in Fiction and MFA in Poetry and teaches at Northern Michigan University. His work has appeared in many journals and anthologies. His collection, *The Mysteries of the Rosary*, was published by Mayapple Press. He has released three spoken word albums with the band Streaking in Tongues. Marty has been nominated twice for the Pushcart Prize and served two consecutive terms as U.P. Poet Laureate. Currently, he is President of the U.P. Poet Laureate Foundation and the Adult Programming Coordinator for Peter White Public Library.

**Jennifer Elen Bríd** (Jennifer Howell) was born and raised in the Upper Peninsula, having lived in Gladstone, Marquette, and the Keweenaw. A musician, writer, non-traditional celebrant, and eclectic solitary practicing Druid, Jennifer endeavors to develop deep ties to the land wherever she roams, celebrating Creation through these conduits of experience. Jennifer plans to relocate to New Mexico, and will carry the blessings of the lakes, forests, people, and experiences in the U.P. within her always. She intends to collaborate with artists in the U.P. while making her way in the vibrant Santa Fe and Taos region.

**B. Harlan Deemer** has lived, since 2019, on the Upper Peninsula, keeping an eye on Lake Huron as it rises and falls. He has self-published two books: *Having Words Together* and *Courting Rejection*.

**Chad Faries** has published two poetry collections, *The Border Will Be Soon* (Emergency Press) and *The Book of Knowledge* (Vulgar Marsala Press). His memoir *Drive Me Out of My Mind,* which chronicles his first eleven years in over twenty different houses across the U.P. and the U.S. at large, was published by Emergency Press in 2011; he is working on a follow-up. Recently he produced an award-winning documentary, *Iron Family,* which follows his sister Jazmine who lives with Down Syndrome and her "double life" through her celebrity plays that she produces every summer in Iron River with the help of the community. Currently he is an Associate Professor of English at Savannah State University.

**Deborah K. Frontiera** grew up in Lake Linden but lived away for many years, teaching kindergarten in Houston, Texas. She returned many summers when her children were young to visit Grandma and Grandpa. She and her husband finally bought their own U.P. summer "fixer upper camp" to spend more time in the U.P. between school years. They became Michigan residents again after retirement, buying a house "up the hill" in Calumet. Their grandchildren come to visit them in the summer. [authorsden.com/deborahkfrontiera]

**Kathleen M. Heideman** is the author of *Psalms of the Early Anthropocene.* She has completed residencies with the National Park Service (including Isle Royale), watersheds, research stations, foundations, and the National Science Foundation's Antarctic Artists and Writers Program. Drawn to wild and threatened places, she works to defend them as a board member of the Upper Peninsula Environmental Coalition. Heideman received a Writer's Award from the City of Marquette and was a finalist for U.P. Poet Laureate. Her work appears in *And Here: 100 Years of Upper Peninsula Writing* (MSU Press). Her manuscript, *A Brief Report on The Human Animal*, won third place in the International 3-Day Poetry Chapbook Contest; it will be published in 2024. Curious woman.

**John Hilden** is an inveterate scribbler from way back. He first picked up a pen in 1966 and hasn't put it down since. Talk about writer's cramp. Someone will probably have to pry it from his cold, dead hand. He lives in south Marquette in a house with many windows on the front. His wife Carolyn and mischief-loving cat Myrtle are the undersong playing beneath the surface of his life.

**Jonathan Johnson**'s poems have appeared in *Best American Poetry* and many literary magazines—including *Ploughshares, North American Review, Prairie Schooner, Missouri Review,* and *Southern Review*—and been read on NPR. He migrates annually between his hometown of Marquette, Michigan; his ancestral village in the Scottish Highlands; and Eastern Washington University, where he teaches poetry in the Master of Fine Arts program and is Head Editor of Willow Springs Books. Johnson hosts *The Poet's Nook* on WNMU Public Radio 90, and his most recent books are *May Is an Island* (poetry) and *The Desk on the Sea* (memoir).

**Kathleen Carlton Johnson** was born in Laurium, and is both a teacher and a visual artist. She has been a fellow at the Anderson Center in Minnesota and the American Academy in Rome. Poetry and language have been lifelong passions. Her work has appeared in *The MacGuffin, 3rd Wednesday, Rattle,* and *The William and Mary Review,* and in every edition of the *U.P. Reader* since 2021. Her current publication is *Rain of Stars: Poems* (Traprock Press). She currently lives in Lake Linden and is a member of Upper Peninsula Publishers and Authors Association (UPPAA), where she writes a column called "Waterproof White" for the organization.

**Ellen Lord** is a U.P. native. She was raised in Ontonagon, Stephenson, and Trout Creek, and has always cleaved to wild places. She is a behavioral health therapist specializing in addiction and trauma. Her writing has appeared in *Bear River Review, Dunes Review, Walloon Writers Review, U.P. Reader, HSA/Frogpond,* and elsewhere. Her chapbook, *Relative Sanity,* is available at several independent bookstores as well as online. Her email address is ellenlordcs@gmail.com. [ellenlordauthor.com]

**Raymond Luczak** (editor) is the author and editor of over thirty books, including U.P.-centric titles such as *Animals Out-There W-i-l-d: A Bestiary in English and ASL Gloss,*

*Far from Atlantis: Poems, Chlorophyll: Poems about Michigan's Upper Peninsula,* and *Compassion, Michigan: The Ironwood Stories.* His collection *once upon a twin: poems* was selected as a U.P. Notable Book of the Year for 2021. Growing up as the only one deaf in a hearing family of nine children, Luczak spent the first eighteen years of his life in both Ironwood and Houghton, Michigan. A proud Yooper native and an inaugural Zoeglossia Poetry Fellow, he resides in Minneapolis, Minnesota. [raymondluczak.com]

**Gala Malherbe** grew up in Munising and lives in Marquette, Michigan. Her parents fostered her connection to nature—camping in the Hiawatha National Forest, hikes along Picture Rocks, weekends at the cabin, blueberry picking along dusty two-tracks, cross-country skiing, and winter campfires. She was truly raised *outside.* She and her husband have raised their own children with full access to the wonder and awe of forest, stream, bog, and lake. In her poems, Gala writes about growing up and living in the U.P. as well as her experiences of parenting, which cannot be separated from the natural world.

**Beverly Matherne**, U.P. Poet Laureate and author of seven bilingual books of poetry, is professor emerita at Northern Michigan University, where she served in the Department of English as director of the Master of Fine Arts program in creative writing and poetry editor of *Passages North* literary magazine. She has garnered seven first-place prizes, including the Hackney Literary Award for Poetry and four Pushcart nominations. Her latest title—*Potions d'amour, thés, incantations / Love Poems, Teas, Incantations*—is from Harvard Square Press. Beverly has relocated across the country many times, but the U.P. is her last stop, her last love.

**R. H. Miller** is emeritus professor of English at the University of Louisville. In addition to his scholarly appearances, he has published a memoir, *Deaf Hearing Boy,* and a chapbook, *A Long Glance.* He has also published poetry, nonfiction, and fiction in several magazines. Although he is not a resident of the U.P., he taught at Michigan Tech from 1961-1964 and has been a constant visitor, and much of his creative work is grounded in the U.P., which he considers his second home.

**Jane Piirto** was born and raised in Ishpeming. She attended Suomi College, graduated from and taught at Northern Michigan University, and is the recipient of a Doctor of Humane Letters from NMU. She is the author of 25 single-authored literary and scholarly books and chapbooks, including *A Location in the Upper Peninsula* (poems, essays, and stories; Sampo) and *Saunas* (poems, Mayapple) and the award-winning novel, *The Three-Week Trance Diet* (Carpenter). A member of the Marquette Poets Circle, she is a retired trustees' professor from Ashland University and lives in Columbus. [janepiirto.com]

**Dana Richter** was raised on a small farm in southern Minnesota. He completed bachelor's and master's degrees specializing in botany and mycology. He moved to the U.P. in 1983 to conduct research, study, and teach forest pathology at Michigan Tech. He has conducted numerous workshops and field trips teaching people about mushrooms and fungi. He has been president of the local bird club and editor of the biannual newsletter for 25 years and is a founder of the Keweenaw Land Trust. His published work appear predominantly in peer-reviewed science journals. He lives on 135 acres north of Hancock spending his days gardening, writing, and making nature observations.

**T. Kilgore Splake** currently lives in a Tamarack Location old mining row house in the ghost copper mining village of Calumet in the U.P. Splake has become a legend in the small press literary circles for his writing and photography. Street Corner Press in Sister Bay, Wisconsin recently published two books about Splake written and edited by Robert Zoschke (*The Road to Splake* and *Splake Eyes*). Splake's most recent book *Escape to the Wild* was published by Wood Thrush Press in Swanton, Vermont.

**Suzanne Sunshower** moved into a tiny, semi-off grid hunt shack in the big woods of Michigan's U.P. when she was sixty. No one had ever lived there year-round before, and the realtor said, discouragingly, "I think you'll find it *very* challenging." Her poems in this anthology reflect her experiences of adjustment during the first year of her big new adventure at Bear Shack.

**Russell Thorburn** is the author of four poetry collections. *Somewhere We'll Leave the World* (Wayne State University Press) draws on his own experiences while imagining fictional characters and personal heroes. In a previous book, *Misfit Hearts*, he chronicles the making of *The Misfits* through the filming-location photographs of Clark Gable, Marilyn Monroe, and Montgomery Clift. In his latest collection *Let It Be Told in a Single Breath* (Cornerstone Press, University of Wisconsin-Stevens Point), he resumes where he'd left off with recurring characters and a younger self in dislocations of time and space. He has received numerous grants, including a National Endowment for the Arts Fellowship, and he was the U.P.'s first Poet Laureate.

# acknowledgments

The editor is grateful to Eric Thomas Norris for his thoughtful insights, Jonathan Johnson for his enthusiastic promotion of all things poetry and the U.P., Adam Kauwenberg-Marsnik for his magical cover photograph, and Tom Steele for his editorial input on the book's foreword.

The memory of David Cummer (1956-2022) continues to be a blessing.

The editor is deeply indebted to Victor R. Volkman for enabling this anthology to happen. Through his involvement with the Upper Peninsula Publishers and Authors Association (UPPAA.org), Victor has done so much to help spotlight the rich literary traditions found in the U.P. experience. Working with Victor is always a great honor.

**Chlorophyll: Poems about Michigan's Upper Peninsula**

For many of those who've lived there, the Upper Peninsula of Michigan can seem like a magical place because nature there feels so potent and, at times, full of mystery. After having grown up there, Raymond Luczak can certainly attest to its mythical powers. In *Chlorophyll*, he reimagines Lake Superior and its environs as well as his houseplants as a variety of imaginary and historical characters.

> Ghosts dress in only gray and white.
> This is how they camouflage their volcanic selves.
> Lake Superior is bottled with them.
> You can't see them but they move like fish ...

"In Raymond Luczak's *Chlorophyll*, the devastating natural beauty of Michigan's Upper Peninsula is imbued with passions its reticent human inhabitants are loathe to express. Trees, lakes, and stones air their infatuations, their grudges, their mythologies and griefs. Through this forest of the otherwise unsaid, we catch glimpses of a speaker who knows there is no line to blur between 'person' and 'nature.'"
—Emily Van Kley, author of *Arrhythmia* and *The Rust and the Cold*

**Available in paperback, hardcover, ebook, and audiobook
from Modern History Press**
Print ISBN: 978-1-61599-642-1